The G.I. Bill, the Veterans, and the Colleges

The G.I. Bill,
the Veterans,
and the Colleges

Keith W. Olson

The University Press
of Kentucky

ISBN: 0-8131-1288-5

Library of Congress Catalog Card Number: 72-91667

Copyright © 1974 by The University Press of Kentucky

A statewide cooperative scholarly publishing agency
serving Berea College, Centre College of Kentucky,
Eastern Kentucky University, Georgetown College,
Kentucky Historical Society, Kentucky State University,
Morehead State University, Murray State University,
Northern Kentucky State College, Transylvania University,
University of Kentucky, University of Louisville, and
Western Kentucky University.

Editorial and Sales Offices: Lexington, Kentucky 40506

To my wife, Marilyn

Contents

Preface

This book has three interwoven subjects: the higher education provisions of the World War II G.I. Bill, the veterans who used them, and the colleges (I have used interchangeably the terms college and university) at which the veterans studied. The emphasis is on group action and attitude, on milieu, and on programs rather than individuals or institutions. Neither the genesis nor the legislative enactment of the G.I. Bill reflected the work of any one or even of several indispensable persons. At the heart of the G.I. Bill operation, moreover, were the veterans and the colleges, and there were over two million of the former and almost two thousand of the latter.

The Servicemen's Readjustment Act of 1944, as the G.I. Bill was officially named, contained six titles, of which only part of one title related to higher education. The first and sixth titles involved procedures and administration, while the fourth covered employment and the fifth unemployment. Home, farm, and business mortgages came under Title Three. Title Two dealt with education and training of all types, at all levels. The veterans who attended college constituted only a minority of veterans who utilized Title Two's provisions.

Despite the bill's several distinct titles, veterans and the public usually associated the term G.I. Bill with education and training benefits, especially in higher education. The image of a veteran attending college, compared to that of a veteran returning to high school or learning a trade, seemed more colorful, more in harmony with the nation's educational aspirations, and easier to romanticize and to publicize in films and writings. If a veteran had difficulty finding a job, by way of contrast, he joined the 52–20 Club ($20 unemployment checks for 52 weeks); if he wanted to buy a house, he applied for a V.A. mortgage. But if a veteran wanted to go to college, he thought of the G.I. Bill.

I selected the University of Wisconsin for a case study because it combined a tradition of academic excellence with service as a state university, exhibited both rural and urban influences, balanced quality undergraduate education with distinguished graduate education, and blended a cosmopolitan atmosphere with localism. Wisconsin's stature as one of the nation's ten best universities, its size, and its progressivism, on the other hand, offset some of its representativeness. Nevertheless, the Wisconsin study presented in detail how one university and its veterans interacted. My research indicated that additional case studies would produce, despite variations, the same general pattern of relationships and essentially the same conclusions.

My association with the G.I. Bill's college program has been favorable, personal, and of long standing. In 1950 my brother earned his undergraduate degree under the World War II act. Four years later I enrolled in college under the Korean G.I. Bill. While an undergraduate I started a clipping file on the G.I. Bill and as a graduate student first considered doing a book-length study. Countless friends, classmates, professors, and professional colleagues studied under the World War II and Korean G.I. Bills. Today I have students registered under the Vietnam G.I. Bill. I have benefited from this first-hand experience.

In addition to acknowledging my debt to the many G.I. Bill veterans I have known, I want to thank publicly the institutions and individuals who assisted me in this study. The U.S. Office of Education provided a year's financial support to start the project, and the General Research Board of the University of Maryland awarded me a summer's grant to finish it. Staff members of the following institutions courteously answered questions, arranged for the copying of material, and aided in my search of sources and information: the American Council on Education, the American Legion National Headquarters, the National Archives, the Franklin D. Roosevelt Library, the Harry S. Truman Library, the University of Maryland, the University of Wisconsin, and the Veterans' Administration Research Division. Mrs. Neva A. Carlson, information specialist in the U.S. Office of Education, located and made available several reports and bulletins. At the University of Wisconsin former president E. B. Fred, director of summer school Clay Schoenfeld, and student organization adviser Peter Bun granted me interviews. Douglas A. Dixon, veterans counselor at Wisconsin, provided access to his office files, answered questions, and made suggestions. The editors of the *Wisconsin Magazine of History* and the *American Quarterly* graciously permitted me to reprint material that first appeared as articles in their journals (Winter 1969-1970 and December 1973, respectively). My colleagues in the History Department at Maryland offered their reactions to chapter one during a faculty seminar. One of these colleagues, Horace Samuel Merrill, read the entire manuscript and improved its style and clarity. And finally, my wife, Marilyn, added to the manuscript's readability and maintained an attitude and atmosphere conducive to research and writing.

1. Origins and Motives

Within the first year of the demobilization process there will exist the likelihood, if not the certainty, of a large volume of unemployed, involving as many as 8 or 9 million.

> Final Report of the Conference on Post-War Adjust-
> ment of Civilian and Military Personnel, June 1943.

The primary purpose of any educational arrangements which we may recommend should be to meet a national need. . . . We have regarded any benefits which may be extended to individuals in the process as incidental.

> Report of The Armed Forces Committee on Post-
> War Educational Opportunities for Service Personnel,
> July 1943.

[The provisions of the G.I. Bill came] largely . . . from the best rehabilitation ideas and procedures developed between 1918 and 1943. . . . The contents were not new.

> Warren H. Atherton, 1943-1944 National Com-
> mander of the American Legion, writing in Novem-
> ber 1967.

AMERICANS traditionally have granted postwar benefits to able-bodied veterans. Colonial legislatures and the British Parliament established the practice with the first settlements. The rebellious colonial legislatures and the Second Continental Congress of the Revolutionary years continued with the policies. No Congress under the Articles of Confederation or the Constitution of 1787, moreover, deviated from this basic principle. The specific benefits able-bodied veterans enjoyed—land grants, cash bonuses, and pensions—depended upon the conditions during and following each of the nation's military conflicts. Often the degree of generosity of the benefits resulted from the successful activity of postwar veteran pressure groups, especially the Sons of Cincinnati, founded after the Revolutionary War, the Grand Army of the Republic, established after the Civil War, and the American Legion, organized after World War I. Since few persons ever have opposed adequate medical care and pensions for disabled servicemen, the enduring political controversy in American history over veteran benefits has been concerned essentially with the rewards demanded for healthy veterans. After the European phase of World War II erupted in September 1939, most Americans realized that American involvement would bring new demands for veteran benefits. It had always been so.[1]

Government concern for the postwar welfare of the men who donned uniforms during World War II arose in the summer of 1940 amidst the debate to increase mobilization and eighteen months before the United States entered the war. This concern mirrored, above all else, the nation's economic condition. That summer, when congressional leaders wrote the first peacetime conscription act in the nation's history, they included a provision to guarantee reemployment rights to all veterans who had left regular jobs to enter the armed forces. The provision helped to reduce hostility to a peacetime draft, initiated a new method by which the government could carry out its obligation to compensate for the interruption of civilian life, and reflected awareness of an unemployment rate during 1940 of almost fifteen percent. Few young men wanted to give up hard-to-find jobs to spend a year in the army and then return unemployed to civilian life. The reemployment provision of the Selective Service Act of 1940 indicated a sentiment in favor of legislation to help veterans during the period immediately after their release from active duty and thus foreshadowed the central theme of the G.I. Bill. Once the United States entered the war in December 1941, President Franklin D. Roosevelt, his executive agency (the National Resources Planning Board), the American Legion, and both houses of Congress recognized the need for a major program to aid all veterans during the nation's demobilization.

Thus the program to send veterans to college can be understood fully only as one aspect of the larger problem of maintaining economic health and political stability during demobilization. During World War I Congress and President Woodrow Wilson had failed to enact legislation to assist able-bodied veterans returning to civilian life. The American Legion, founded in 1919, insisted that the veteran had been slighted, and championed a veteran bonus to correct the injustice. In the process the American Legion became an important political pressure group. For fifteen years the veteran bonus question endured as a political issue of consequence: a result of veteran pressure, vetoes of bonus bills by four presidents, a march by veterans on Washington, and the eventual payment.

The role that unemployed European veterans had played in the rise of fascism instigated an element of fear in the thinking of many Americans. They wondered what American veterans would be like when they returned from military life, especially if they could not find jobs. Meanwhile, the ever-present specter of economic depression hung over the nation and shaped what observers later called a depression mentality. Intensifying anxiety over these three ghosts of the past were the unprecedented millions of servicemen answering roll call each morning. The sheer numbers of future veterans frightened Americans. Leaders across the country influenced others to believe that something had to be done for the veterans—something beyond a bonus, something that would contribute significantly to a healthy economy, and something that would allay veteran resentment toward government. Ideally, a well-paying, meaningful job available for each veteran would solve the problem. This solution, however, was not viable. The years since 1929 had demonstrated that capitalism could not maintain full employment without massive federal intervention or without continued giant outlay for military spending. The executive branch of government seemed particularly aware of this situation.

To chart a postwar reform movement, Roosevelt turned to the National Resources Planning Board (NRPB), the agency he called "the planning arm of my Executive Office." [2] Established by executive order on 1 July 1939, the NRPB consolidated and succeeded several federal planning agencies (the first of which Congress created in 1931) interested in national resources, the economy, and public works. Roosevelt appointed his uncle, Frederick A. Delano, as head of the agency to generate and coordinate ideas and plans. In January 1940, Roosevelt asked the agency "to study the transportation system of this country and to outline what that system, including railroads, highways, pipelines and airways, may or should look like ten years hence." [3] Through its eleven regional offices the NRPB undertook studies of river basins for potential development similar to that of the Tennessee River Valley. In addition to an annual report the NRPB published special studies, such as "The Economic Effects of the Federal Public Works Expenditures, 1933–1938," which appeared in 1940. [4] Pearl Harbor did not significantly alter the work of the NRPB. "Post-defense planning" merely became "post-war planning."

Roosevelt placed great importance on the NRPB's work. On 14 January 1942, nine days after his annual budget message, he transmitted to Congress the "Development of Natural Resources—Report for 1942," prepared by the NRPB. He declared his intention of "establishing the custom of an annual planning report as a companion document to the Budget of the United States." [5] The heart of the report was a nine-point declaration of principles, drafted with Roosevelt's participation. To the old Bill of Rights, "to the old freedoms," the report emphasized that "we must add new freedoms and restate our objectives in modern terms." These new freedoms included "the right to fair pay, . . . the right to adequate food, clothing, shelter and medical care, . . . the right to education, . . . [and] the right to equality before the law." [6]

By its very nature, then, the NRPB considered as a matter of course postwar problems and the needs of individuals whose lives the war had reoriented. On 1 July 1942, Delano requested Roosevelt to approve his suggestion to appoint "a small planning committee" to analyze problems of "the demobilization of men in the armed forces and industry" and to counter such problems by preparing "a comprehensive program with recommendations." Delano added that the NRPB already had "discussed this matter with the Federal agencies concerned" and felt that "early agreement upon a comprehensive well-articulated program" would be a morale boost to the young men whose lives had been interrupted. Roosevelt half agreed. "This is no time for a public interest in or discussion of post-war problems," he replied, because such activity "includes the danger of diverting people's attention from the winning of the war." Although he ruled out publicity, Roosevelt saw "no harm in a wholly unpublicized, 'off the record' preliminary examination of the subject . . . but without any form of an official set-up." He wanted "no committee as such" but suggested Delano "ask four or five people . . . to work on this in their spare time in order that they may be better prepared for an official study and report and recommendations later on." [7]

The committee Delano appointed held its first meeting on 17 July and called its work the "Conference on Post-war Readjustment of Civilian and Military Personnel," often shortened to 'Post-war Manpower Conference" (hereafter cited as PMC). Between July 1942 and April 1943, the group conducted twenty-seven half-day sessions chaired by Dr. Floyd W. Reeves, a consultant to the NRPB since June 1941, a staff member of the American Council on Education (ACE), and a professor on leave from the University of Chicago. Among the twelve members of the PMC were Brigadier General Frank T. Hines, Administrator, Veterans' Administration; Dr. A.F. Hinrichs, Acting Commissioner of Labor Statistics, Department of Labor; Dr. Francis J. Brown, member of the ACE and Education Adviser to the Joint Army-Navy Committee on Welfare and Recreation; and Colonel Francis T. Spaulding, Chief, Education Branch, Special Service Division, War Department, and former Dean of the Harvard Graduate School of Education.[8] The PMC members shared the common experience of dealing with manpower statistics on the national level.

The committee discussed personnel demobilization topics such as the coordination of military discharges and employment opportunities, the agencies best suited to administer a demobilization program, the economy and manpower requirements of postwar America, and the educational needs of the labor force. Lacking the staff, time, authorization, and need to do otherwise, the PMC drew its information and ideas from the agencies its members represented (especially the NRPB), from their remembered experiences of World War I, and from the demobilization plans of Canada.

For the first meeting Reeves mimeographed a "Suggested Agenda" which started with three basic assumptions: 1) 'Military demobilization cannot be considered independently of the re-employment program for civilian employees in business, industry, government and the professions"; 2) the transition from a war to a postwar economy "requires retaining a substantial proportion of wartime workers both civilian and military"; and 3) "Any training program must be planned in close articulation with vocational counselling, placement, and the general demobilization programs of the armed services and industry." The three-page agenda, which placed as much emphasis upon retraining civilians as it did upon retraining veterans, also proposed that the government pay a subsistence allowance "for reasonable periods of time in approved training programs."[9] Reeves' agenda echoed the spirit and work of the NRPB, formed the central themes with which the PMC worked, provided the conceptual framework of the group's final report, and aroused no opposition at the meeting.

Past experiences with veterans and with veteran programs consistently guided the PMC. General Hines, for example, recalled that the armistice of World War I found the nation unprepared for demobilization, and he therefore considered the committee's work "second only to the question of winning the war," because "the greatest danger was that of having idle veterans drifting aimlessly about the country in search of non-existent jobs."[10] Members of the committee agreed with Hines. They seriously debated holding men in service rather than creating a period of heavy unemployment and increased expenditures for relief. Committee members who had previously dealt with veterans recounted the World War I rehabilitation law of 1919 which provided tuition, fees, books, and a subsistence allowance of $90 to $145 a month for the vocational and professional training of disabled veterans. Although limited to a minority of all veterans, the program established the principle of rehabilitative aid for a few years with the intention of returning veterans to remunerative occupations.

On 31 July 1942, Lieutenant Colonel Edward A. Fitzpatrick, who often attended meetings with General Hines, distributed a confidential eight-page report titled "The Wisconsin Educational Bonus Law of 1919," which bore strong similarities to the educational program the committee suggested in its final report. The Wisconsin legislation provided each state resident who had served three months prior to 1 November 1918, $30 a month for four academic years to attend any nonprofit elementary or high school, technical institution, college, or university in the state. If no school offered the exact program a veteran desired, he could select a school in another state. The State Board of Education administered the program, but the question of admission and instruction remained a matter between the school and the veteran.

In October 1942 the NRPB published a six-page pamphlet, "Canadian Preparations for Veterans' Demobilization and Rehabilitation," which described among other features a clothing allowance, unemployment insurance, land settlement, educational benefits, and business assistance.[11] Under the Canadian plan, veterans who had their education interrupted received fees and a monthly maintenance allowance (ranging from $60 for a single veteran to $138 for a veteran with a wife and six children) for a period determined by their length of service. The plan also permitted veterans to pursue postgraduate work in approved cases. Passed in October 1941, the Canadian law provided another education model for the committee. Several committee members traveled to Montreal in March 1943 to meet with the Joint Economic Committee of Canada and the United States to discuss postwar planning. A month later the NRPB brought Brigadier General H. F. McDonald, chairman of the Canadian Committee on Demobilization and Rehabilitation, to Washington to attend meetings and to advise the PMC.[12]

The PMC's final report in June 1943, "Demobilization and Readjustment," also known as the "Report of the Conference on Postwar Readjustment of Civilian and Military Personnel," won unanimous endorsement from its members. Many of its ninety-six proposals were generalities and only indirectly touched the lives of individuals. Number ninety, for example, recommended that the program outlined "be considered as the national minimum," while proposal ninety-one suggested that the federal government coordinate its activities with state governments. Other proposals were more precise. One called for three months' furlough at regular pay (not to exceed $100 per month) and family allowances for all servicemen at the termination of their active duty. Another stipulated twenty-six weeks of unemployment insurance for veterans. Proposal after proposal, indeed the heart of the report, dealt with education and training and their relationship to employment.

The rationale for the proposals reflected what the committee believed the postwar years would bring. According to the committee's conclusions, the postwar economy would be depressed. From the war's peak total of 63.5 million jobs, the number would decrease to 57 million jobs. From full employment, "the number of those unemployed might at one stage in the readjustment period be as large as 8 or 9 million," with "the prospects of 3 million persons being unemployed . . . two years after the war." The report warned that "once mass unemployment comes into existence, it is not easily dissipated or dissolved." Wages, hours, and prices, moreover, would "likely . . . return to the levels of 1939 or 1940." With such a view of the postwar period perhaps it was only natural for the committee to propose and to justify educational programs essentially in a utilitarian light.[13]

The committee outlined a two-part plan for the education and training of servicemen. First, a general plan which offered twelve months of schooling at any level, designed to refresh persons for old jobs or to equip them for altered or new jobs was open to all veterans. Second, a supplementary plan would provide an additional three years of education for a select number of veterans whose education had been interrupted by the war or who "had made unusual progress or who otherwise could be shown to have particular aptitude and ability." The supplementary plan would be administered under a competitive system of scholarships and structured "to encourage the education of men for technical and professional occupations in which there are likely to be shortages of adequately trained personnel." No scholarships would be offered "in fields in which there is already an over-supply . . . or in which there is little likelihood of satisfactory and useful employment." Scholarships would be made available in proportion to the rate of demobilization and their number increased should unemployment develop. Both plans would pay tuition and fees for veterans as well as maintenance allowances, unspecified in amount except that they should be modest enough to attract only the serious veteran. Without going into detail, the report designated the United States Office of Education to administer the program.[14]

The report also pointed out the need for a limited vocational training program "for workers displaced from employment because of demobilization and the termination of war contracts, to equip them for employment in peacetime industry." As in the case of the veterans' supplementary education plan, the training of workers would "be confined to occupations in which there is an unsupplied demand . . . and to new trades and occupations." Although the committee believed the subject to be outside its province, it called attention to the educational needs of young workers who, had they not been drawn into war industry, would "have continued their education in schools, high schools, or colleges." If all the programs the PMC recommended were implemented, the report estimated the cost would be between $3.5 and $7 billion, depending upon conditions.[15] The NRPB "strongly" endorsed the report of its special committee, and Roosevelt, after reading its 106 pages, concluded that it "carries one step further the specific proposals of the NRPB" which he had "submitted to the Congress on March 10, 1943."[16]

Roosevelt never regarded the work of the Post-war Manpower Conference as more than preliminary, informal, and exploratory.[17] Although they knew he wanted no publicity, the committee members persistently pressured Roosevelt to issue a formal public statement about manpower demobilization and readjustment in the postwar period.[18] Roosevelt, just as persistently, refused. On 13 November 1942, however, the day he signed into law the amendment to the Selective Service Act lowering the draft age to eighteen, Roosevelt had announced that a presidential "committee of educators, under the auspices of the War and Navy Departments," would study the program needed to enable "the young men whose education has been interrupted to resume their schooling and afford equal opportunity for the training and education for other young men of ability after their service in the armed forces has come to an end." [19]

The President made his announcement for several reasons. He wanted a report from the PMC describing the scope and the nature of the problems the country would face during demobilization. When the NRPB established the PMC it intended to present Roosevelt with such a report sometime between mid-October and the end of the year. Instead, at the meeting of 8 October 1942, the PMC admitted it had bogged down and a month later still wondered if it would accomplish its objective. After the 8 October meeting, members of the NRPB discussed with Roosevelt the PMC's slow progress. Roosevelt decided to move in another direction. On 22 October he sent to Robert P. Patterson, Undersecretary of War, a draft of the statement he planned to make on 13 November and directed Patterson to clear it with representatives of the navy. He also asked Patterson for suggestions of persons to serve on a new committee. Roosevelt worried about the military. During the fall of 1942 neither the army nor the navy expressed an interest in demobilization plans. Roosevelt, who had served as Assistant Secretary of the Navy during and following World War I, often remarked about the lack of planning for that earlier period and wanted to avoid repeating the neglect. By involving the armed forces in the new committee, Roosevelt reasoned, he would force the army and navy into planning. And finally, considering the public's opposition to drafting teenagers, Roosevelt executed a wise political move. He acknowledged that many of the new draftees would have to interrupt their schooling and promised to make amends by having the government help them resume their education after the war.

To head this new study group, called The Armed Forces Committee on Post-war Educational Opportunities for Service Personnel, Roosevelt appointed Brigadier General Frederick H. Osborn, Director of Special Services Division, Army Service Forces. Named to serve under Osborn were Cortlandt C. Baughman, Director of Special Activities, Bureau of Naval Personnel; Rufus C. Harris, president of Tulane University; Dexter M. Keezer, Deputy Administrator, Office of Price Administration; Young B. Smith, Dean of Columbia University Law School; and John W. Studebaker, United States Commissioner of Education.

The Osborn Committee performed several functions. Unlike the PMC, it devoted full attention to one aspect of readjustment—education for veterans. Harris and Smith provided higher education with official spokesmen and Studebaker provided the same representation for the United States Office of Education. It forced the army and navy into cooperation on postwar planning. And finally, it informed Americans of the government's continued interest in veterans. Roosevelt, with these good reasons for establishing the Osborn Committee, did not expect and did not want the new committee to duplicate the work on education already completed by the PMC.

When Roosevelt asked Osborn to direct the new study group he explicitly stated that "the Committee should correlate its activities with the related studies of the National Resources Planning Board," and "use them so far as possible." [20] Osborn carried out Roosevelt's directive. He designated as his assistant Colonel Francis T. Spaulding, chairman of the education subcommittee of the PMC, who immeditely became secretary of the Osborn Committee. Captain Baughman selected as his assistant Lieutenant Commander Ralph A. Sentman, also a member of the PMC. The chairman of the PMC, Floyd Reeves, attended the meetings of the Osborn Committee and worked "in close cooperation" to coordinate the activities of the two groups.[21] Consequently, the Osborn Committee met for the first time on 18 January, for the second time on 22 February, and never met more than once a week. It submitted its major report in July 1943.

As could be expected, the recommendations of the Osborn Committee differed only in a few details from those made about education by the PMC. Osborn's committee report required veterans to have had at least six months service to be eligible for benefits, while the PMC settled for three. Unlike the PMC, the Osborn Committee suggested specific amounts, $50 for single and $75 for married veterans, for the monthly maintenance allowances. The Osborn Committee recommended commencement of study within six months of discharge and the PMC set its limit at one year. For the selection of students for supplemental education, the Osborn Committee suggested a quota system for states, while the PMC wanted recipients picked on a national competitive basis. And to help the supplemental students, the Osborn Committee proposed a loan program.[22]

The rationale of the Osborn Committee proposals indicated no concern for individual veterans as such. "We have regarded any benefits which may be extended to individuals in the process as incidental . . . . The primary objective . . . of all the efforts of our committee," the report emphasized, "is to do what is necessary to overcome the educational shortages created by the war." To assist the nation in reaching this objective, the report favored early discharges for "young men and women who have clear-cut and feasible plans to get ahead with their education," and for "competent young teachers and administrators." The Committee estimated the total cost of the program as "approximately" one billion dollars.[23]

On 28 July 1943, Roosevelt read a fireside chat to the nation on the progress of the war and on plans for peace and thereby made his first approach to Congress about veteran benefits. He declared that veterans "must not be demobilized into an environment of inflation and unemployment, to a place on a bread line or on a corner selling apples." He asked Congress to "do its duty" to prevent such conditions, enumerated minimum veteran benefits (mustering-out pay, unemployment insurance, government-financed education or training, credit in the Social Security program for years spent in service, and adequate medical care and pensions), and added that he planned to recommend specific legislation "within a few weeks."[24] Roosevelt could and did provide some of the necessary oratory, but he needed help to draft legislative proposals. This he did not have. During the next three months every cabinet department and every federal executive agency demonstrated that it lacked either the time, the sympathy, or the initiating precedent to draft legislation for veterans.[25] The NRPB expired on 31 August because thirteen months earlier, on 26 June 1942, Congress had voted to abolish the organization by withholding funds. Venting its hostility to federal economic planning, Congress had ordered further that the NRPB's functions could not be transferred to any other agency. Thus, while Roosevelt lamented and Congress approved, no federal agency moved to fill the planning vacuum.[26] Meanwhile, the number of bills in Congress to aid veterans increased; the American Legion started a concerted drive for effective legislation; the talk about a bonus became more frequent; and the mood of the nation seemed to support the idea of legislation for veteran benefits. And, as a presidential aide warned Roosevelt's friend and adviser, Harry Hopkins, in the summer of 1943, "unless something is done soon on the legislation of returning soldiers, the opposition may steal the thunder." [27]

Three months after his fireside chat, Roosevelt still lacked an agency or committee to give organization, direction, and life to his proposals. Consequently, he sent to Congress the Osborn Committee report he had received in July. He had no real alternative. By October 1943 the PMC and its parent, the NRPB, no longer existed, though the Osborn Committee still could function if needed. Congress, of course, had demonstrated its opposition to economic planning when it abolished the NRPB. If Roosevelt wanted to plan for the postwar-era, veteran benefits constituted the one feasible method, particularly educational provisions. Congress had made Roosevelt's postwar planning more difficult, and with the war raging and elections a year away the President lacked the time and the inclination for a confrontation on this issue.[28] Roosevelt admitted that the Osborn Committee report was only "a helpful and constructive point of departure in the working out of a practical program," and indicated his reasons for wanting legislation. He felt that the nation was "morally obligated to provide this training and education," and that the legislation would be "conducive to the maintenance of high morale" among servicemen. Roosevelt asserted that "the welfare of the Nation itself" required a correction of the educational deficit the war had caused. He believed that the money invested would "reap rich dividends in higher productivity, more intelligent leadership, and greater human happiness."

A month later, Roosevelt resurrected several PMC proposals and asked Congress to enact measures providing for veteran mustering-out pay, unemployment insurance, and credit in the Social Security program for the years spent in service.[29] Several factors forced Roosevelt to present recommendations for a series of bills for veterans in the autumn of 1943 and later to make recommendations for demobilization in general, rather than present one comprehensive measure. First, the PMC had experienced early difficulty in designing a broad, unified program of demobilization. In addition, Congress had abolished the NRPB and had created a planning vacuum. Finally, Roosevelt was in danger of losing political advantage if he did not suggest legislation. His foremost recommendation, embodied in the Osborn Committee report, dealt with education.

Meanwhile, by October 1943 the dominant representatives of the nation's educational community, headed by the American Council on Education, had produced a plan of veteran benefits that generally agreed with the Osborn report. The ACE was a nonprofit organization of educational associations and institutions of higher learning founded in 1919 for the improvement of education, with particular emphasis on higher education. Cooperation between the ACE and federal planning agencies dated from the 1930s. George F. Zook, president, and Francis J. Brown, staff member, for example, both prepared reports on education for the National Resources Committee, the predecessor of the NRPB. Floyd W. Reeves, a staff member of the ACE, became consultant to the NRPB with responsibility for postwar planning for education. He prepared the sections on education in the NRPB's annual reports, chaired the PMC and worked hand-in-glove with the Osborn Committee.[30] From the beginning of the war the ACE had concerned itself with postwar education for veterans. In January 1942 the NRPB's subcommittee on education, with the cooperation of the ACE, sent questionnaires to over 1,800 colleges and universities to discern occupational shortages.[31]

The ACE worked closely with the PMC and the Osborn Committee.[32] During the summer of 1943 the ACE submitted to its members, which included more than 600 colleges and universities and almost all the nation's professional educational organizations, a questionnaire soliciting opinions regarding educational programs for veterans. On 16 August 1943, the ACE sent every member of Congress a summary of its questionnaire. Two months later, and eleven days before Roosevelt sent the Osborn Committee recommendations to Congress, Zook sent to Samuel I. Rosenman, Roosevelt's principal speech writer, a two-page proposed plan of veteran benefits drafted by the ACE's Committee on Relationships of Higher Education to the Federal Government. The members of this ACE committee had met since early summer. The list of committee members resembled a who's who of higher education; it included the presidents of the University of California, Indiana University, Harvard University, Tulane University, Cornell University, and the University of Wisconsin. Zook made it clear that despite the Committee's orientation toward higher education, it had gone to "considerable pains to consult other members of the council whose field of work is on the elementary, secondary, and vocational level," and that the committee's conclusions represented "the ideas of educational organizations, and individuals, almost unanimously." [33] Unlike the Osborn report, which stated precisely the reason behind its plan, the ACE never indicated whether it recommended its program primarily as a reward to honor veterans, as a device to replenish the nation's stock of educated citizens, as a means to prevent unemployment, or as a method to help educational institutions.[34] Since the ACE and individual educators had worked closely with the PMC and the Osborn Committee, the overwhelming agreement on principles and details between the educators and the executive branch of government came as no surprise.

In their recommendations regarding education neither the PMC, the Osborn Committee, the President, nor the educators moved beyond a blend of "The Wisconsin Educational Bonus Law of 1919," the

Canadian benefits for veterans, and the extension to able-bodied veterans of the program established by Congress in 1919 for the education and training of disabled servicemen of World War I. Roosevelt and the members of both committees shared the primary motivation of practical concern about the postwar economy, but on this matter educators were not specific. When Congress took up the question of sending veterans to college, therefore, it started with widely supported plans characterized in scope and motive by moderation, not by idealism and boldness.

Congressional consideration of educational benefits for veterans lasted from November 1943 to June 1944, involved the American Legion in a decisive role, and stayed within the broad outline drafted by the Osborn Committee. The legislative history of the G.I. Bill in Congress, from proposal to enactment, followed the pattern similar to many bills. On 3 November 1943, Senator Elbert D. Thomas, former political science professor and loyal New Dealer from Utah, introduced a bill incorporating the Osborn-Roosevelt recommendations. The Senate referred the bill to its Committee on Education and Labor, headed by Thomas, which in turn assigned it to a subcommittee. Thomas held hearings from 13 to 15 December and favorably reported the bill to the Senate on 7 February 1944.

Meanwhile, during the autumn of 1943, the American Legion initiated a campaign to write a competing, more comprehensive bill. On 23 September 1943, the American Legion, at its twenty-fifth national convention, adopted a resolution directing its national executive committee to appoint a special committee to draft a rehabilitation program for veterans. In various other resolutions the convention voted that any master plan should include adequate medical care, unemployment compensation, education and vocational training, home and farm loans, and a system of furlough pay to soften return to civilian life. After several meetings of the executive committee, National Commander Warren H. Atherton carried out this mandate. On 30 November he appointed John Stelle (former state treasurer, lieutenant-governor, and for three months Democratic governor of Illinois) chairman of the committee and added seven prominent Legionnaires to serve with him.[35]

Stelle's committee held its initial meeting in Washington on 15 December. After consulting with various leaders of labor, business, education, government, and military, the committee and its assistants wrote a comprehensive bill with titles covering hospitalization, employment, unemployment, home and farm loans, business loans, mustering-out pay, education, and administrative procedures. The day after the committee finished its first draft, Jack Cejnar, the Legion's acting director of public relations and a former newspaper man, labeled the master plan the G.I. Bill of Rights. Short and graphic, the name easily caught the imagination of Congressmen, servicemen, and the public and conveyed just the right touch of emotion.[36] On 9 January 1944, the Legion released its omnibus bill to the press.

When Congress reconvened the following day, after its annual Christmas-New Year's recess, John Rankin, Democrat from Mississippi, and chairman of the House Committee on World War II Veterans' Legislation, introduced the Legion bill. The next day, Joel Bennett (Champ) Clark and nine other Senators, representing both parties and all geographical regions except the Far West, sponsored the bill in the Senate. Clark, a border-state Democrat from Missouri and the Legion's first National Commander (1919), provided indispensable skill and commitment in navigating the bill through the Senate's legislative shoals.

The Senate Finance Committee, through its Subcommittee on Veterans' Legislation, conducted nine days of hearings on Clark's bill between 14 January and 10 March. On 13 March, Clark introduced a new bill embodying the same provisions, clarified and amended. It deleted the title for mustering-out pay, because Congress had passed a separate mustering-out bill which Roosevelt had signed on 3 February. The new bill, written in large part by the Legion and incorporating important features of the Thomas bill, enjoyed the unprecedented sponsorship of eighty-one Senators. Clark, the Legion, and the war were convincing. On 18 March the Senate Finance Committee unanimously reported the new Clark bill to the Senate and six days later the Senate sent the omnibus bill to the House with a fifty to zero vote.[37]

At the time the Senate sent the Legion's bill to the House, the measure's section on education generated the most debate. Comparisons between the popular Legion bill and the administration-sponsored Thomas bill were common, with the greatest attention focused on the choice of the federal agency assigned to administer the benefits. The Thomas bill, with the unanimous support of educators, called for the U.S. Office of Education to direct the program, while the Legion bill, with strong endorsement from the Veterans' Administration and from Senators and representatives who were veterans of World War I, quite naturally assigned the authority to the V.A.[38] Other differences in the two bills also sparked discussions. The Thomas bill included veterans of the Merchant Marine under its benefits while the Legion bill did not. The Thomas bill would pay all fees and tuition; the Legion bill would limit fees and tuition to $300 a year. The Thomas bill included a ten-dollar monthly subsistence allowance for each dependent child of the veteran; the Legion bill did not. But whereas the Thomas bill required six months of service for eligibility, the Legion bill demanded only ninety days. A Thomas bill provision entitled all veterans to a year's study and allowed a small percentage to receive three more years; the Legion bill restricted benefits to veterans whose education or training had been interrupted, but offered to all members of this group four years of schooling. These collective differences, important as they were, did not prevent compromise.

Once in the House, the Legion bill rested in the hands of Rankin, who maneuvered the bill into his own committee and then conducted hearings for thirteen days between January and March, ending with several days of testimony on Clark's bill after it had passed the Senate. After an Easter recess, Rankin's committee met in executive sessions nineteen times, amended the Senate's bill in a number of instances, and on 3 May reported favorably to the House. On 18 May, following several days of debate, the House approved its version of the G.I. Bill without a dissenting vote. The joint Senate-House conference committee, appointed to iron out the differences, presented a compromised version of the bill on 12 June and by the next day both Houses approved. President Roosevelt signed the bill into law on 22 June 1944.[39]

The final education title provided one year of schooling for veterans who had served at least ninety days and who were not over twenty-five years old at the time of entry into service. Veterans were eligible for an additional period of education beyond the first year, equal to the time they had spent on active duty. Thus a man who served two years could attend college for a year under the first provision and for two additional years under the second. Veterans over twenty-five at the time they donned uniforms had to demonstrate that their education had been impeded or interrupted. In no event could a veteran's schooling exceed four years. The act also included payment of all fees, tuition, books, and supplies up to a maximum of $500 per school year and authorized payment of a monthly subsistence allowance ($50 for single and $75 for married veterans) while in school. Under this law the V.A. determined whether the veteran was eligible for benefits, the veteran selected the school of his choice, and the school evaluated his qualifications for admission. About the only restriction the veteran encountered was the requisite to enroll at an institution accredited by the state education agency of the state within which the school operated. The law read further that "no department, agency, or officer of the United States, in carrying out the provisions . . . shall exercise any supervision or control, whatsoever, over any State educational agency . . . or any educational or training institution." [40] In this area there had never been anything but agreement among politicians, Legionnaires, and educators. Everyone had worked to avoid the slightest trace of federal control over education.

From the time it first publicized its G.I. Bill to the day of Roosevelt's formal approval, the American Legion supplied the driving force that made legislation possible. The Legion found its task relatively easy because almost all participants and interested observers shared similar apprehensions about veterans and the economy in the postwar period. In its work for legislation the Legion made two fundamental contributions—an effective lobbying effort that included writing the actual bill and the idea of combining a list of diverse benefits into a package deal. Both contributions reflected a superior grasp of the political situation and a more aggressive leadership than that offered by Roosevelt or Congress. The Legion's masterful campaign on behalf of its omnibus bill exhibited well-conceived strategy and a wide range of tactics, including use of radio, movies, petitions, newspapers, and personal appeals. One episode of the campaign involved enough color and drama that NBC recreated it on a half-hour program, "The March of Time." Looking back twenty-five years later, Legion Commander Atherton recalled that "the material . . . the G.I. Bill committee and I" selected "for inclusion in the Bill" came largely "from the best rehabilitation ideas and procedures developed between 1918 and 1943. . . . The contents were not new. They were born of many decades of sacrifice, suffering, trial and error." [41] John Steele, chairman of the committee that wrote the Legion bill, likewise claimed no originality. "We are taking," he remarked on 29 March 1944, "several bills and several thoughts of the Members of Congress and the President of the United States and trying to get together legislation for the benefits of . . . veterans." [42] With the exception of the loan provisions, the Legion bill did not deviate from the proposals and ideas previously expressed by the Roosevelt administration during the autumn of 1943. [43] The idea of an omnibus bill, however, represented a new method of offering familiar recommendations, proved an astute political move, and contrasted sharply with Roosevelt's piecemeal approach.

The Legion worked hard not to offend Roosevelt and repeatedly insisted that its bill carried out his suggestions of October and November

1943. When Clark opened hearings on the bill on 14 January, he called Atherton as his first witness. Near the end of his testimony, Atherton commented that the Legion was "glad that the views expressed by the President are so close to what we conceive to be the proper aid and assistance to these men." [44] That afternoon, Atherton, Stelle, Clark, and the other nine Senators who introduced the Legion bill, spent forty-five minutes discussing veteran legislation with Roosevelt. Clark reported to newsmen after the meeting that the President favored comprehensive legislation but that Roosevelt had failed to comment specifically about the Legion bill.[45] Roosevelt's aides recognized that the Legion bill, "if given the legislative right of way, would result in the sidetracking of the Thomas education bill," which the administration had initiated.[46] With bipartisan support of the Legion bill, with general, personal agreement toward the measure, and with no meaningful alternate proposal, Roosevelt remained aloof, letting the Legion keep the initiative.[47] When Roosevelt signed the bill on 22 June 1944, he remarked that it "substantially carries out most of the recommendations made by me in a speech on July 28, 1943, and more specifically in messages to the Congress dated October 27, 1943, and November 23, 1943." [48] The Legion, of course, always claimed that the G.I. Bill embodied its own proposals. Both were correct, but this fact should not minimize a basic difference between Roosevelt and the Legion. Roosevelt viewed veteran benefits as an important campaign for a successful demobilization program, but he knew other battles lay ahead. The Legion, on the other hand, felt its work did not extend beyond the veteran. With passage of the Servicemen's Readjustment Act of 1944, therefore, it considered its basic legislative action finished. At the signing of the G.I. Bill, however, Roosevelt reminded the Legion and the nation that "apart from these special benefits which fulfill the special need of veterans, there is much to be done [for reconversion and readjustment]." [49]

Roosevelt's willingness to suggest and later approve legislation to assist able-bodied veterans indicated a complete departure from the position he firmly held during his first term. In a speech before the American Legion national convention on 2 October 1933, Roosevelt enunciated the principle "that no person, because he wore a uniform, must therefore be placed in a special class of beneficiaries." Nineteen months later, when he vetoed a veterans' bonus bill, Roosevelt emphasized that the able-bodied veteran "should be accorded no treatment different from that accorded to other citizens who did not wear a uniform." [50] Roosevelt left no explicit statement explaining why he changed his position toward veterans, but the magnitude of the war, and thus the intensity of the problem of demobilization and the sense of obligation, probably had a lot to do with it. Ever the politician, Roosevelt also recognized the political advantage of his new position. On 20 July 1944, when he accepted the Democratic nomination for President for a fourth time, Roosevelt told the party faithful that the voters in November would decide about leaving the "task of post-war reconversion to those who offered the veterans of the last war breadlines and apple-selling . . . or whether they will leave it to those who . . . have already planned and put through much legislation to help our veterans."A month later, Roosevelt's running mate, Harry S. Truman, described veterans as the "most potent" voting group in the country. And two months later, Samuel Rosenman wrote to Roosevelt, "It might be well to release this letter from General Osborn in order to remind people that you started this whole business for veterans' education." [51] Obviously, a politician could find voter favor by helping veterans; the unanimity of congressional approval of the G.I. Bill already had indicated that.

The Legion's straight-forward desire to reward veterans had several origins. Above all, the Legion felt veterans had "earned certain rights to which they are entitled. Gratuities do not enter the picture." [52] Veterans, the Legion maintained, "should be aided in reaching that place, position, or status which they had normally expected to achieve and probably would have achieved, had their war service not interrupted their careers." Inseparable from this sincere desire to help was blended a second, broader reason. Supporting the G.I. Bill in a radio speech the evening of 2 May 1944, Atherton warned the American people that veterans "will be a potent force for good or evil in the years to come. They can make our country or break it. They can restore our democracy or scrap it." In a similar mood, past commander Harry Colmery saw "troublous times . . . ahead," and reminded the House Committee on World War Veterans' Legislation "that after the last war, except for England, this is the only country where the men who wore uniforms did not overthrow the government on either side of that conflict." Throughout their speeches and writings, Legion leaders told "how the veterans of the first World War were shoved around during the lush years of the twenties," and insisted that the process not be repeated. Using symbols of the 1930s, Atherton thundered, "We do not want our sons and daughters selling apples on street corners." *The National Legionnaire* demanded that "there must be no road hereafter from the battle-line to the bread-line for our defenders!" [53]

The Legion's reasons for wanting legislation coincided with the views expressed by other public figures. Eleanor Roosevelt, for instance, warned as early as April 1942 that the veterans might well create "a dangerous pressure group in our midst" and to blunt this threat the government would have to "adjust our economic system so that opportunity is open to them on their return, or we may reap the whirlwind."[54] While Congress weighed the merits of the G.I. Bill, Maury Maverick, chairman and executive director of the Smaller War Plants Corporation and noted for his liberalism, told the Commerce and Industry Association of New York that if returning veterans could not find jobs the country might move into "a dictatorship."[55] In the same vein, Republican Congressman Hamilton Fish, from Roosevelt's home district in the Hudson Valley of New York State and known for his conservatism, admonished his House colleagues that World War II veterans would not "come home and sell apples as they did after the last war, because if that is all they were offered, I believe we would have chaotic and revolutionary conditions in America."[56] And when the Senate Finance Committee unanimously recommended the G.I. Bill to the Senate in March 1944, it prophesied in its formal report that "if the trained and disciplined efficiency and valor of the men and women of our armed forces can be directed into the proper channels, we shall have a better country to live in than the world has ever seen. If we should fail in that task, disaster and chaos are inevitable."[57] In 1944, when the Legion constantly reviewed the previous quarter century and used descriptions of many of its undesirable features to generate support for its legislation, it merely confirmed the thinking and analysis of most political observers. Few challenged the Legion's reading of history or its proposals designed to avoid reliving it.

Several veteran groups, while agreeing with the Legion's outline of history, placed a different emphasis on the past, however, and thus provided the most important opposition to passage of the G.I. Bill. On 16 February 1944, while both congressional committees were studying the bill, Omar B. Ketchum, national legislative representative of the Veterans of Foreign Wars; Frank Haley, national representative of the Military Order of the Purple Heart; Millard W. Rice, national service director of the Disabled American Veterans; and W. M. Lloyd, national commander of the Regular Veterans Association, sent an open letter (addressed to Senator Clark) to every member of Congress. They questioned "whether this so-called G.I. Bill of Rights, in its entirety, is a sound and equitable solution to the problems and needs of World War II veterans." These men singled out the title on education

as "so broad in scope and potential cost, that its enactment would
. . . probably not only prevent any consideration of several other
more equitable proposals to solve such problems, but might also
subsequently jeopardize the entire structure of veteran benefits and
provoke another Economy Act [of March 1933]." The country's first
responsibility, they continued, rested with the disabled. Reminding
Congress of their organizations's 550,000 members, the four officials
cautioned Congress "not to be stampeded into hasty and possibly
unwise legislation." [58] The letter marked the high point of veteran
opposition to the Legion bill and clearly indicated that the opposition
had its roots not in any defects of the bill or its objectives, but in
fear that by carelessness disabled veterans might suffer, as they had
in the past. In January 1944, for example, Rice emphasized that his
organization favored "all of the benefits" listed in the Legion's bill,
and three weeks after the open letter to Clark even specified that
the DAV did "not object to the education" title.[59] Haley of the MOPH
felt much the same. A month after he signed the open letter, Haley
testified before the Rankin Committee that the education title went
too far because it "would have a tendency" to kill "the goose that
laid the golden egg." Otherwise, he explained, the Legion has a "splendid
bill." [60] The Legion and the VFW, moreover, cooperated throughout
the winter and spring of 1943 and 1944 to effect legislation.[61] But
like Haley and Rice, Ketchum wondered about the generosity of the
education title, and, unlike the Legion, still believed in the feasibility
and merit of a bonus. Early in March, therefore, Ketchum's VFW
joined four other veteran organizations to sponsor a bill for "adjusted
compensation." [62] When the idea failed to gain momentum, Ketchum
moved into closer step with the Legion and gave full support to the
G.I. Bill. The MOPH and the DAV, alone, ineffectual, and haunted
by the ghost of scarcity, opposed the bill to the end.

From the beginning educators, especially those associated with
the American Council on Education, shared in the planning, drafting,
and evaluating of the G.I. Bill. They served as members of, or consultants
to, the PMC, the Osborn Committee, the congressional committees,
and the American Legion, yet they never worked as prime movers.
The educational community, as Dr. George Zook often remarked,
supported the educational title almost to a man, with the exception
of those who wanted the U.S. Office of Education, not the V.A., to
administer the program. In several areas—tuition, subsistence allowance
for children, national rather than state quotas for additional education,
and abolition of the link between educational benefits and employment

opportunities—educators worked to liberalize both the Osborn-Roosevelt-Thomas bill and the Legion bill. They proved successful almost in direct proportion to the degree that their desires matched those of the Legion. Educators showed little willingness to fight for a plan granting all veterans four years of schooling. The ACE plan submitted to Roosevelt in October 1943 incorporated the principle that educational benefits beyond a first year should be limited to a select group of veterans. During the late winter and spring, when Senator Burnet R. Maybank of South Carolina and Congressman Graham A. Barden of North Carolina attempted to liberalize educational opportunities, the ACE sponsored a conference of "the representatives of 21 of the most important national [educational] organizations in this country." This conference endorsed the idea that all veterans should receive four years of schooling.[63] But the statement of Roscoe L. West, president of the American Association of Teachers Colleges, indicated the cautious nature of many educators. Speaking "for the executive committee" of the AATC and "as a member" of the ACE's Committee on Relationships of Higher Education to the Federal Government, West agreed with Zook that the federal government should not make educational loans to veterans because "we think it might be difficult to collect." West also could "see no reason why their [veterans] total [educational] expenses should be paid under any situation."[64] In general, however, the educational community considered the question of which federal agency would administer the program far more vital than the question of who should receive the benefits and for how long.

The origins and motives for enactment of the G.I. Bill revealed a widespread awareness of the past and an attempt to ward off a recurrence of undesirable conditions and events. The title of the act announced the intent of its supporters to help the veteran readjust to civilian life. But the persons responsible for the legislation clearly indicated by their statements and testimonies that the primary problem lay with the economy, not the veteran. Almost everyone realized that war spending had ended the depression that had lasted throughout the 1930s and that during the war the nation had enjoyed the rarity of full employment. Politicians and other leaders had little faith that the economy could sustain this full employment as it moved from war to peace,[65] yet they were convinced that the United States could not safely allow extensive veteran unemployment. If the man in uniform would go from the battle line to the breadline, the common theme ran, he probably would demand radical economic and political changes.

The fear of unemployed veterans, not the fear of maladjusted veterans motivated the persons who enacted the G.I. Bill.

At its root, the Servicemen's Readjustment Act of 1944 was more an antidepression measure than an expression of gratitude to veterans. To prop up the postwar economy Congress could have poured money into corporations, as it did in the 1930s through the Reconstruction Finance Corporation; it could have created jobs, as it did during the New Deal through such programs as the Works Projects Administration and the Civilian Conservation Corps; it could have curtailed the profit motive and moved toward a planned economy, as the Scandinavian democracies had done. Instead, Congress chose to stimulate the economy through the veterans. The economy needed federal help; the veterans served as a convenient, traditional, and popular means to provide that assistance. Anxiety over economics preceded and dominated altruism toward veterans.[66]

Samuel Rosenman later insisted that Roosevelt "conceived" the G.I. Bill,[67] while the leaders of the Legion asserted that "the Legion conceived it; the Legion drafted it, and fought for it." [68] Both deserved credit, of course. Roosevelt's executive agency first produced proposals for veteran legislation, but the Legion took the initiative, drafted a bill, and lobbied it through Congress. Although Congress conducted hearings and modified proposals, it played, in general, "a reactive rather than initiative role" in passage of the act.[69] Above all, however, the G.I. Bill was a child of 1944; it symbolized the mood of a country immersed in war, recalling the depression, and worrying about the future.

2. Anticipation and Preparation

Colleges and universities will find themselves converted into educational hobo jungles. And veterans, unable to get work and equally unable to resist putting pressure on the colleges and universities, will find themselves educational hobos.. . . education is not a device for coping with mass unemployment.

> Robert M. Hutchins, President of the University of Chicago, December 1944.

Postwar committees, appointed on almost every campus, have been quietly and effectively preparing. . . . Reconversion in higher education cannot be a return to prewar policies, procedures, curricula, and methods of instruction.

> Francis J. Brown, Consultant, American Council on Education, October 1945.

As WORLD WAR II neared its conclusion, more and more Americans turned their thoughts to what veterans would be like and what they would do with their lives when they returned from military service. Ironically, those who worked with the G.I. Bill prior to its passage seemingly pondered little about the expected behavior of veterans, except to agree that unemployed veterans would threaten the political and economic status quo. However, during the first two years following passage of the act many government officials, educators, veterans, and interested observers were apprehensive in their descriptions of the would-be student-veteran. They often underestimated the maturity of veterans as students and consistently underestimated the numbers of servicemen who desired a college education. Meanwhile, educators worked to adjust their academic programs to the needs of the veterans. At the same time veterans and their friends pressured Congress to liberalize the educational title of the G.I. Bill.

Considering the magnitude of its later operation, the G.I. Bill received little notice when President Roosevelt signed it into law on 22 June 1944, and the act continued for many months to receive less attention than hindsight would deem appropriate. Although Roosevelt honored the signing of the document by having his picture taken with members of Congress and the American Legon looking over his shoulder, such papers as the *New York Times*, Washington *Post*, Baltimore *Sun*, Chicago *Daily Tribune*, New Orleans *Times Picayune*, *Los Angeles Times*, *San Francisco Chronicle*, and *Des Moines Register* did not consider the legislation worthy of an editorial. Four months later, the *New Republic* felt it necessary to interpret the essence of the act. "Contrary to popular belief," the editors wrote, "this bill does not proclaim a special, inalienable Bill of Rights for veterans. Rather, it is to facilitate, as quickly as possible, the readjustment of veterans to civilian life." An Army study conducted in October 1944 among white enlisted men stationed within the United States indicated that "their knowledge of the educational provisions of the 'G.I. Bill of Rights' is still scanty and inexact. . . . It is quite probable that men serving overseas have even less information about it." The study concluded that "thus far, the G.I. Bill of Rights has not been an outstanding factor in the decision to return to school."[1]

From 1944 to 1946 numerous authors with varying backgrounds published books about veterans and their postwar readjustment, in hopes of capitalizing on the general interest in and glorification of servicemen. These authors differed widely in their awareness of the

G.I. Bill's education title and its potential value. Columbia University sociologist Willard Waller concluded in 1944 that veterans would be indifferent to education, but he nevertheless favored maximum use of education because it provided "the shortest route to real rehabilitation." The classroom, Waller insisted, was "the best place for many, if not most of the younger veterans." [2] Charles G. Bolte, chairman of the American Veterans Committee, writing a year later, agreed with Waller about the lack of veteran interest in education, but he did not share Waller's desire to overcome this indifference. Veteran apathy toward education, Bolte reasoned, meant "that the best provision of the bill will never be useful to the great majority of veterans." [3]

While some writers from 1944 to 1946 devoted short chapters to education in all its phases, others ignored the subject.[4] Journalist Morton Thompson, a veteran himself, blended humor, satire, and advice in an attempt to make the best-seller list with a book about veteran adjustment to civilian life. He apportioned entire chapters to "How to Talk Civilian" and "How to Get in Bed with Your Wife," but included no mention of veteran education. Certainly the idea of an ex-marine wearing a freshman beanie, a thirty-year old playing college football, or a young coed being simultaneously wooed by a fuzzy-cheeked teenager and a twenty-four-year-old former fighter pilot contained exceptional material to satirize. But satire has no point unless it is associated with widely shared experience or knowledge. When Thompson wrote, Americans apparently lacked a coherent image of the student-veteran. Had such an image existed, Thompson and others probably would have used it. In February 1945, eight months after passage of the G.I. Bill, Penguin Books published a volume, *Psychology for the Returning Serviceman*, prepared by a committee of the National Research Council and intended to help veterans adjust to civilian life. Although the authors included chapters about "Choosing a Job" and "Learning New Skills," they failed to mention the G.I. Bill.[5] Nevertheless, two months later the book went into a second printing.

There were several reasons why the G.I. Bill initially attracted little attention. Compared to war measures, domestic legislation seemed unimportant, especially legislation designed for the future. When Roosevelt signed the G.I. Bill, news of the Allied invasion of Europe, then only two and a half weeks old, dominated the news and made the postwar era seem remote. Another explanation for the G.I. Bill's reception stemmed from its lack of direct precedent. In 1944 and 1945 Americans lacked a clear understanding of what the legislation meant. They could conceptualize a new Volstead Act or a new WPA measure, but not a G.I. Bill. Perhaps the public would have been more aware of its existence had the legislation gained passage after a bitter political controversy. The G.I. Bill, of course, had become law without a dissenting vote in Congress.

Although the general public overlooked or underestimated the G.I. Bill, many educators and army personnel gave the act their attention and prepared for its implementation. They concentrated on the question of participation under the education title, because the number of veterans involved under this title would determine the major cost of the program, would confront higher education with an unusual challenge, and would serve as a social and economic safety valve. Supporters of Title II believed that many veterans would not be able to find work unless they were better trained or educated. They also predicted that if unemployment were high, veterans would return to school rather than remain idle. The supporters of Title II, therefore, expected that a favorable response to the bill would mean a healthier economy and a more stable society.

No one associated with the G.I. Bill, or specifically with its education title, believed that the legislation would be an economic panacea. The appeal of the G.I. Bill lay in the fact that it would help the economy and at the same time do something for the veterans. But it was only a partial answer. In August 1944, six weeks after the passage of the G.I. Bill, President Roosevelt, for example, worried about "the postwar employment," and told James F. Byrnes, who served as unofficial assistant president, that his "first thought is that something like the CCC program could be instituted." But, he continued, "the more I think of it the more convinced I am that the time has come to press for the Universal Training Bill in one form or another," with the participants "paid as were the CCC boys—$30 a month with the bulk of it going back to their families straight." [6]

The War Department conducted three surveys to estimate the number of veterans who would return to the classroom after the war. During the summer of 1943, starting soon after the National Resources Planning Board submitted to President Roosevelt its final report on the postwar needs of veterans, the Research Branch of the Morale Services Division, Army Service Forces, "queried a representative cross section of white enlisted men throughout continental United States" and found that seven percent planned to return full time to school or college after the war. A government subsidy to veteran students, the survey's analysts concluded, would increase only to eight percent the number of servicemen who wanted to resume a student's role.

The War Department logically emphasized that the findings could not "be taken as an accurate forecast of what the attitudes will be at the end of the war," but since the findings constituted the only available guidelines, officials used them. On 2 January 1944, for example, while the Senate Committee on Education and Labor considered his proposal for a G.I. Bill, Senator Elbert D. Thomas told a newspaper reporter that about seven percent of servicemen could be expected to apply for educational benefits if they were available.[7]

The Information and Education Division of the Army Service Forces conducted the second and the third surveys, both of which had greater depth than the first. The second survey took place in the summer and autumn of 1944 and sampled the intentions of officers and enlisted men, black and white. It reported that "the best prediction of the number of men who will return to full-time school is in the neighborhood of 8 percent." Conducted during the summer of 1945, the third survey encompassed two studies, "one of white enlisted men in service at twelve installations in the continental United States in August, and the other a survey of men being released from separation centers in July." The main findings led "to a prediction that a minimum of eight percent and a maximum of twelve percent of all veterans of Army service in World War II will attend full-time school or college." With navy veterans added, the survey concluded that "at least a million veterans [will enroll] in schools and colleges within six months to a year after demobilization is complete."[8]

The three army surveys of soldiers' attitudes toward postwar education were the only broad samplings taken during the war, and they served as the basis for the flood of enrollment predictions that filled the writings and discussions about the course of postwar higher education.[9] Most members of the press accepted the army's statistics and passed them on to their readers, but some observers questioned the findings and offered clarification.[10] In December 1944 President Roosevelt vaguely estimated the number of veterans who would return to the classroom as "hundreds of thousands." That same month when Frank T. Hines, administrator of the Veterans' Administration, wrote to James F. Byrnes, director of the Office of War Mobilization, he cast doubt upon surveys in general. "It has been our experience," Hines recorded, "that a survey, if it could be made at this time, would not reflect what the veteran will do when the war is over." The next month Hines shed his usual cautiousness and publicly estimated that a total of 700,000 veterans would become college students, but since that number would "be distributed over several years," he felt existing academic facilities were adequate.[11] In March 1945 Earl J. McGrath, a World War II veteran and a dean at the University of Buffalo, published his analysis of the army's statistics. McGrath had served as a specialist in higher education for the American Council on Education and as education adviser to the Chief of Navy Personnel; he later became a U.S. Commissioner of Education. Drawing upon his own experiences and the army's study, McGrath concluded "that in no academic year will more than 150,000 veterans be full-time students in colleges and universities." Enrollment increase from veterans, he continued, would be "from 10–15 percent," with a total of 640,000 attending under the legislation.[12] William Mather Lewis, president of Lafayette College, speaking at the annual dinner of the National Institute of Social Sciences, insisted "that the number of men who will avail themselves of educational offerings of the G.I. Bill of Rights is being overestimated."[13] In August 1945, Stanley Frank, who regularly wrote about veterans and other subjects for the *Saturday Evening Post*, published an article titled "G.I.'s Reject Education," in which he used early veteran enrollment to conclude that the G.I. Bill "is a splendid bill, a wonderful bill, with only one conspicuous drawback. The guys aren't buying it."[14]

The response to the three army surveys, then, was one of general acceptance with some assertions that projected enrollments were excessive. Rarely did anyone argue that the army findings underestimated future veteran registration on the nation's campuses.[15] Colleges and universities, the consensus indicated, could expect to enroll about two-thirds of the million veterans who wanted additional formal education or training. Frank T. Hines, Benjamin Fine (the education editor of the *New York Times*), and others pointed out that enrollment would fluctuate according to the unemployment rate. Hines predicted an increased enrollment of fifty percent if jobs were scarce. Fine felt that if unemployment were high, "the rush to colleges would be tremendous, . . . [perhaps] as many as a million veterans."[16] When Hines and Fine indicated a direct relationship between unemployment and educational enrollment, they reiterated a familiar conclusion, expressed first by the Post-War Manpower Conference in 1942.

The opinions expressed about the expected performance of veterans as students varied more widely than did enrollment predictions, with the balance tipped toward anxiety rather than confidence. Above all else the differences of opinion seemed to reflect the experience and personalities of the authors. Writing for the general reader, Dixon Wector, a prominent historian who had made a special study of veterans, concluded about the veteran that "one thing is sure. As he went forth, so he will return: friendly, generous, easy-going, brave, the citizen-soldier of America." Another prominent professor, Columbia University's Willard Waller, also writing for the public, came to an opposite conclusion: "No man can fight in a war without being changed by that experience. Veterans are glad to come home, but they come home angry." [17] Numerous observers concluded that veterans would reject their military experiences (in this case discipline) and rebel against authority, while other observers felt that veterans would accept their military experience (in this case training) and flock to "practical" courses.

The educators and other observers who felt veterans would be exceptional students cited such assets as added maturity, increased initiative, greater sense of purpose and social consciousness, and wider experience.[18] The persons who viewed the veteran with a wary eye worried about veteran restlessness, a lack of initiative, and hostility toward authority.[19] Some commentators, believing the gap too great between seasoned veterans and new high school graduates, raised the question of segregating veteran and nonveteran students, and a few colleges debated the merits of such segregation.[20] Others pointed out that veterans, tired of dogmatic, impersonal, and uniform military instruction, would need to be handled with unusual care in the classroom. Edward C. McDonagh, a professor on military leave serving as an occupational counselor at an army separation center, for example, offered some advice to his colleagues. He advised professors "to find out as much as possible about the military backgrounds, assignments, and ranks" of their veteran students, and "to be cautious in praising one branch of the Army to the exclusion of others." He also recommended making courses interesting, relevant, and humorous. In deference to veteran resentment of orders, McDonagh added that "it may be wise to offer . . . 'suggested' reading" or "voluntary aids," rather than required assignments.[21]

Members of the academic community felt a special concern for the educational challenges of providing a satisfactory curriculum and environment for the veterans. "The old-style liberal education," warned Donald A. Stauffer, an ex-marine returning to his professorship of English at Princeton, "will be under constant bombardment." A sense of urgency and a stress on functional training, both the result of their military experience, meant that "the great majority of veterans will desire vocational, technical, and professional training," Francis J. Brown reported for the American Council on Education.[22] A host of educators joined in the chorus that Stauffer and Brown sang.[23] Another problem was the married student. Before the war, marriage provided grounds for expulsion in many colleges because tradition held that marriage and college did not mix. When the army conducted its surveys to determine the postwar education plans of its men, it indicated that married men, along with men past twenty-four and men out of school more than a year prior to entering the service, were "quite unlikely to return to a school" despite their stated desires and plans. Sociologist Waller remarked that marriage "is a reason for thinking twice or perhaps thrice before entering college. . . . If there is a baby, college is almost out of the question for any reasonable man . . . . [even with] sufficient outside income." A University of Chicago dean, A.J. Brumbaugh, would accept married veterans but asked, "in all seriousness . . . . What will we do with married students on the campus? How will we house them? . . . Will we be embarrassed by the prospect of babies and by their arrival?" [24]

Two of the country's most prominent educators, meanwhile, recorded their disapproval of what they predicted would be the general influence of veterans on higher education. James B. Conant, president of Harvard University, found the original act "distressing" because it failed "to distinguish between those who can profit most by advanced education and those who cannot." His ideal G.I. Bill would have financed the education "of a carefully selected number of returned veterans." Reflecting a distrust of colleges and universities to maintain academic standards, Conant feared that because of the G.I. Bill "we may find the least capable among the war generation . . . flooding the facilities for advanced education." 25

The University of Chicago's brilliant but controversial president, Robert M. Hutchins, took essentially the same position as Conant, but he expressed it in harsher terms and before a larger audience. Writing for *Collier's* in December 1944, Hutchins titled his article about the G.I. Bill and higher education, "The Threat to American Education." Although he praised "the principle that there must be no relation between the education of a citizen and the income of his parents," Hutchins viewed the G.I. Bill's educational provisions as "unworkable." He predicted that colleges, in order to increase their income with government-guaranteed tuition payments, would admit unqualified veterans and would not expel veterans incapable of doing college work. Colleges, he prophesied further, would keep students longer than "actually required" and would "train more men in a given skill than can get jobs in that skill." Hutchins, who opposed in general the vocational orientation of higher education which he felt the G.I. Bill accelerated, concluded the act would "demoralize education and defraud the veteran." The persons who wrote these "absurd"provisions, he reasoned, did so "because they did not think of them as educational provisions at all, but as a method of keeping the veterans off the bread line." [26]

The academic community realized from the start that the student veteran, whether mature scholar or hostile drifter, would be different from the teenager fresh from high school, and they planned accordingly. Though educators varied widely in predicting enrollment and describing veteran characteristics, they were nearly unanimous on the need for and general outlines of the administrative and academic changes required. Professors and administrators early and logically established two common, perhaps inescapable, principles. They planned to treat the ex-serviceman as a student first and as a veteran second, thus absorbing him as much as possible into the normal student body and campus routine. The educators also adopted the principle of flexibility in dealing with the veteran and his program.

Planning for the postwar era started in many places. In June 1943 the American Council on Education reported that according to its survey of 340 colleges and universities, 245 had functioning postwar planning committees.[27] A year later, when Congress passed the G.I. Bill, practically every institution of higher learning in the country had such a committee. Because these committees dealt with a wide range of problems—fund raising, faculty, buildings, and others—most colleges created a second "postwar" committee to handle only veteran affairs. Long before the war ended, professional associations also had committees actively engaged in postwar planning. In 1944 the Southern Association of Colleges and Secondary Schools published a collection of articles titled *The Southern College in the Post-war World;* the American Academy of Political and Social Sciences devoted three-quarters of a volume (January 1944) to "Some Postwar Problems"; and the American Council on Education started to compile a *Guide to Colleges, Universities, and Professional Schools in the United States* to inform veterans of the changes made by the host of college postwar planning committees. On 1 January 1945, the U.S. Office of Education published its initial issue of *Higher Education,* designed to provide "a suitable medium of communication with American colleges and universities," and automatically sent copies to appropriate administrators. The need for planning was obvious and immediate, because servicemen disabled early in the war appeared on campuses under rehabilitation measures long before Congress passed the G.I. Bill for able-bodied veterans.

At the suggestion of their veterans' committees, almost all colleges and universities modified their admission policies to admit by examination veterans who had not graduated from high school and to provide those with serious educational deficiences the opportunity to complete high school on campus or at least to finish their work through correspondence courses. Most schools gave veterans preference over non-veterans in admissions,[28] but perhaps the ultimate of admission flexibility came when women's colleges such as Vassar, Russell Sage, Finch, and Sarah Lawrence admitted male veterans. Colgate, on the other hand, authorized the wives of veterans to attend its formerly all-male classes.[29]

Institutions, guided by the American Council on Education, demonstrated equal flexibility by granting credit for military experience and training. Beginning in 1944, the ACE published and distributed in cooperation with the army and navy *A Guide to the Evaluation of Education Experiences in the Armed Services.* Originally published in loose-leaf form and expanded as material became available, the guide appeared in a completed edition in 1946. It described each of the almost 800 separate training courses taught by the armed forces, and recommended whether completion of the course entitled the serviceman to academic credit and, if so, at what level and how much. George P. Tuttle, registrar at the University of Illinois, directed the committee that produced the guide. He listed nineteen professional associations as supporting and cooperating, including seven accrediting associations. A poll of academic deans in 1948 revealed that ninety-nine percent of their institutions granted credit "for experience, training, or education in the armed services" and that of this number ninety-four percent did so "for the formal service courses as classified in Tuttle's *Guide.*" Of the institutions (fifty percent) which granted credit for the General Educational Development Tests developed by the United States Armed Forces Institute (USAFI), seventy-eight percent followed the recommendations of Tuttle's guide.[30] According to one survey, eighty-eight percent of institutions accepted credit earned by USAFI correspondence courses (approximately one million men took one or more courses). One-hundred percent granted credit for specialized training programs (such as the navy's V-12). Ninety-two percent accepted work completed at the Army University Study Centers.[31] Without Tuttle's guide colleges and universities still would have granted credit for various military training and experience, but the evaluation would have been a more difficult and less satisfactory process.

Beyond evaluation and acceptance of what may be called military transfer credit, institutions occasionally awarded credits strictly on the basis of military service. This blanket credit invariably could fulfill only elective credit, rarely exceeded fifteen hours, usually would not be given in addition to military transfer credit, and often consisted only of exemption from required physical education courses.

Almost all schools adjusted their calendars and curriculums to accommodate veteran enrollment. Institutions that normally offered summer sessions, and some that did not, made it possible to earn a full semester's credit during the summer. Some colleges and universities (and specific colleges within some universities) moved to a three-semester, year-round program. Many schools inaugurated short courses to allow veterans to enroll at times other than the traditional beginning of semesters. For example, veterans could enter Tufts University on the first of each month, while New York University permitted veterans to start any Monday morning.

Curriculum changes took many forms, the most common being the creation of refresher courses. The vast majority of institutions, including law and medical schools, offered these courses in a wide range of subjects, usually for no credit and for periods of less than a semester. Colleges and universities, as a rule, permitted those veterans not interested in formal majors to ignore departmental divisions in selection of courses. Other changes varied from campus to campus: The Wharton School of Finance and Commerce at the University of Pennsylvania established a special sixteen-month course for veterans who felt they could not devote the normal amount of time required; Princeton University and the University of Pittsburgh, for the same reason, instituted the Associate in Arts degree, awarded after four semesters of work; Yale University organized the "Yale Studies for Returning Servicemen," centered on two distinct courses; Harvard's Graduate School of Business waived its degree requirement for veterans; and Oberlin College invited its graduates to return for a year's reorientation.

In addition to changes in curriculum, calendar, credit evaluation, and admission, educators realized that veterans required special services from their schools.[32] Practically every institution, therefore, established a veterans' counseling office to help veterans choose a program of study commensurate with their aptitudes, interests, and capabilities. To assist with the mechanics of housing, finance, and adjustment, colleges and universities created veterans' service offices, which in turn often published a veterans' manual or handbook. While educators worked to liberalize campus procedures and programs, Congress labored to liberalize the G.I. Bill.

On 19 December 1945, the Senate shouted its approval of a number of amendments to the education title of the G.I. Bill and thereby climaxed a nine-month campaign.[33] The amendments, among other modifications, removed the restriction that limited veterans over twenty-five years old to one year of schooling (unless they could prove the war had interrupted their education), they lengthened the time period within which a veteran could initiate and complete his education, and they also raised monthly subsistence allowances from $50 to $65 dollars for single veterans and from $75 to $90 for veterans with dependents.

The campaign for revision arose from the need to adjust subsistence allowances for inflation and from the need to bring the G.I. Bill into closer harmony with the demands of veterans themselves. Support for increased subsistence payments came from numerous sources, including the press, veteran organizations, educators, and politicians. An article in the *New York Times* in the autumn of 1945, for example, revealed that Great Britain and Canada paid higher subsistence allowances than the United States. A *New Republic* editorial characterized the American payments as "ridiculously small," warned that the success of all titles of the G.I. Bill hung in the balance, and concluded that if the program failed, "the consequences are not pretty to contemplate." [34] On 8 October 1945, General Omar N. Bradley, the new administrator of the Veterans' Administration, testified before the Senate subcommittee considering the amendments that because of the increased cost of living he favored higher subsistence payments.[35] Congressman A. Leonard Allen of Louisiana, voicing a popular sentiment, supported the increases because he did not "expect these veterans who have gone through everything over in the Pacific and the Atlantic to have to work their way through school a part of the time." [36] With strong support and weak opposition, the only question about subsistence payments was the amount of the increase.

Groups that championed higher subsistence payments also demanded liberalization of the act. Concerning the twenty-five-year age limit, the American Legion repeatedly thundered, "Why discriminate?" Educators asserted that the proposed amendments would remove "major obstacles to veterans' education." The Veterans of Foreign Wars, the Legion, and the V.A. all reported that their organizations received more complaints about the education provisions than any of the other titles of the G.I. Bill, except for the loan title.

During the drive to liberalize educational benefits, the veterans' organizations played roles similar to the ones they played in passage of the act. The Legion launched its campaign in April 1945, lobbied intensively, and later claimed credit for the victory. Once again, Frank Haley, representing the Military Order of the Purple Heart and speaking for a small percentage of veterans, asked Congress "to repeal the entire act," and Millard W. Rice, national service director of the Disabled American Veterans, insisted "categorically" and "emphatically" that the government had "let down" the disabled veterans. A new organization, the American Veterans Committee, founded eighteen months earlier, advertised its goals of "a more democratic and prosperous America and a more stable world," and used in support of revision the familiar imagery of "soup kitchens and apple-selling." [37] Although Joel Bennett (Champ) Clark had lost his party's election for renomination in September 1944 and was no longer a Senator, the Legion found numerous other friends in the Senate, including Warren G. Magnuson of Washington, Edwin C. Johnson of Colorado, and Claude D. Pepper of Florida. The White House quietly approved but offered no leadership.

Edward E. Odom, solicitor of the V.A., reminded the House Committee on World War Veterans' Legislation that the amendments were not in keeping with the original intent of the act. "The two main purposes of the legislation," he explained, were to offer a year's refresher or retraining course and additional schooling for those whose education had been interrupted, and also "to ease the postwar readjustment period, by reducing the job demand." [38] Correspondence courses, he reasoned, ran counter to these two purposes. He also added that the V.A. opposed removal of the twenty-five-year age restriction, partly because the V.A. had never rejected an over-age veteran's claim that his education had been interrupted. Odom, of course, was right; the amendments of December 1945 did alter the intent of the G.I. Bill. Whereas the central impulse behind the original education title emphasized readjustment of the veteran and of the economy, the impetus behind the education amendments arose from a desire to reward veterans. Odom's evaluation of the legislation and its amendments raised fundamental questions as to the objective of the act and its relationship to higher education, much the same as Conant's and Hutchins's assessments had done earlier. During 1944 and 1945, however, few persons seemed interested in such intellectual pursuits; the questions remained unanswered. When the veterans' groups, led by the Legion, consistently and vociferously preached the righteousness of helping veterans as an end in itself, few politicians and few Americans could or wanted to disagree.

Thus, the response to the G.I. Bill during its first two years did not establish easily defined patterns. Despite low enrollment projections and conflicting analyses of anticipated veteran behavior and performance as students, colleges and universities generally adjusted their policies and programs while the war still raged around the world. The adjustments resulted from, above all else, an application of common sense and later proved how few academic changes really were needed to accommodate veterans. The public and the veteran, meanwhile, seemed to interpret the G.I. Bill more as a bonus to individuals than a program to ward off depression or revolution. To argue against this view and in favor of the original intent of the legislation as an adjustment measure, politicians and educators had to swim against a powerful tide of sentiment. Few had the desire. Finally, the initial reception of the G.I. Bill's education title created demands for amendments whose objectives deviated from those of the majority of the bill's original supporters. And the program in full operation reached proportions even more unexpected.

3. The Pleasant Surprise

When the G.I. Bill was made a law of the land it is probable that no one in his wildest flights of imagination anticipated that veterans would attend college in such numbers as has proved to be the case.

> John S. Allen, Director of Higher Education, New York State Education Department, November 1947.

. . . here is the most astonishing fact in the history of American higher education. . . . The G.I.'s are hogging the honor rolls and the Dean's lists; they are walking away with the top marks in all of their courses. . . . Far from being an educational problem, the veteran has become an asset to higher education.

> Benjamin Fine, Education Editor, *New York Times*, November 1947.

THE VETERANS who took advantage of the G.I. Bill during the latter half of the 1940s distinguished themselves by their numbers, their maturity, and their achievement. They overshadowed their nonveteran classmates, dominated American campuses, and surprised prognosticators. Faculty and administrators, overcoming caution and even fear, hailed them collectively as the best college students ever. Undeniably, they differed more from the students they succeeded and preceded than has any generation in the history of American higher education.

Initially, only a small number of veterans appeared on campuses with letters of acceptance from admission offices and with certificates of eligibility for G.I. Bill educational benefits from the V.A. During the first year of the program 8,200 servicemen entered the academic ranks, and by November 1945 their numbers had increased only to 88,000.[1] The trickle, however, became a flood as the millions of discharges during the fall and winter of 1945–1946 and the liberalization of benefits in December swelled the flow of college-bound veterans. Thanks to flexible admission practices, 125,000 new veterans registered in February 1946 alone, which, when added to the 88,000 enrollees of March, more than doubled the total registration of the program's first nineteen months. By fall, over a million former servicemen crowded onto the nation's campuses. Ten years later, when the last student had received his last check, the V.A. (of whom 64,728, or 2.9 percent, were women) counted 2,232,000 veterans who had attended colleges under the G.I. Bill.[2]

Veterans broke every conceivable enrollment record and made the unusual commonplace. By the fall of 1947, at the peak of veteran enrollment, the number of males registered and the percentage of persons eighteen to twenty years old enrolled in colleges had more than doubled the prewar records; total college enrollment, greater by over a million, had climbed by seventy-five percent. For three years the majority of all male students were veterans and one semester veterans came within a fraction of a percentage point of being the majority of all students. Rutgers University enrollment, for example, soared from its prewar 7,000 to nearly 16,000 students by 1948. Stanford University's number of students jumped from 4,800 to 7,200, and yet its admission office rejected two qualified candidates for every one it accepted. The University of Maine, Boston College, the University of Georgia, and a host of schools of all sizes and descriptions doubled their prewar peak enrollments.[3] Greatly expanded enrollments were not new to colleges and universities in 1946–1947, but the size of

Table 1

ENROLLMENT IN HIGHER EDUCATIONAL INSTITUTIONS, FALL SEMESTERS,
1939–1960

Year	Total Enrollment	Male Enrollment	Veteran Enrollment†		
			Number	% of Total	% of Males
1939	1,364,815*	815,886*			
1945	1,676,851†	927,662†	88,000	5.2	9.5
1946	2,078,095	1,417,595	1,013,000	48.7	71.5
1947	2,338,226	1,659,249	1,150,000	49.2	69.3
1948	2,403,396	1,709,367	975,000	40.5	56.9
1949	2,444,900	1,721,572	844,000	34.4	48.8
1950	2,281,298	1,560,392	581,000	25.2	37.0
1951	2,101,962	1,390,740	396,000	18.7	28.3
1952	2,134,242	1,380,357	232,000	10.8	16.7
1953	2,231,054	1,422,598	138,000	6.1	9.6
1954	2,446,693	1,563,382	78,000‡		
1955	2,653,034	1,733,184	42,000‡		
1956	2,918,212	1,911,458	1,169‡		
1960	3,582,726	2,256,877			

Source: With noted exceptions, Kenneth A. Simon and W. Vance Grant, *Digest of Educational Statistics 1968* (Washington: Government Printing Office, 1968), p. 68.

*Opening (Fall) Enrollment in Higher Education, 1960: Analytic Report, U.S. Office of Education, OE–54007–60, Circular No. 652 (Washington: Government Printing Office, 1961).

†U.S., Congress, House, *The President's Commission on Veterans' Pensions, A Report on Veterans' Benefits In the United States, Staff Report IX, Part B: Readjustment Benefits: Education And Training, And Employment And Unemployment,* 84th Cong., 2d sess., 1956, H. Print 291, p. 26.

‡Veterans Administration Monthly Report, November 1954, November 1955, and November 1956.

the increase both in absolute numbers of students and in the percentage increase during such a brief period were unprecedented. Few observers had predicted such increases, but even if they had done so, the war and postwar shortages of building materials would have prevented an adequate building program to accommodate the students. The manpower and teacher shortage likewise blocked a satisfactory solution to personnel problems that the giant enrollments created. In contrast, officials and educators preparing for hordes of students of the 1960s studied birth rates and educational statistics to predict the numbers and to plan for the additional students who swarmed on campuses during that decade. Comparable planning had not been possible for the veteran students of 1946–1950.

Institutional enrollments varied. With tuition paid by the government, veterans attempted to enter the best institutions their records would permit. In the fall of 1948 the majority of veteran men enrolled in privately controlled institutions, while the majority of nonveteran men registered at publicly controlled institutions.[4] Veterans flocked to the Ivy League schools, the state universities, and the better liberal arts colleges and technical schools. They enrolled only as a last resort in junior colleges, teachers colleges, and lesser-known, small liberal art schools. At the opening session of the Association of American Colleges Conference in January 1946, educators reported that the smaller liberal arts colleges still had room for 250,000 veterans, while at the same time the better-known and larger institutions were turning away qualified veterans. Harry S. DeVore, president of Central College (Fayette, Missouri) stated that his enrollment was 250 below the normal prewar figure of 600 students, and the president of DePauw (Greencastle, Indiana), Clyde E. Wildman, remarked that his registration was only eighty percent of its peacetime 1,500 students.[5] Meanwhile, administrators at Syracuse University and the University of Michigan prepared their campuses for record-shattering enrollments for the spring semester. Forty-one percent of all veterans that spring registered at thirty-eight institutions, with the remaining fifty-nine percent scattered among 712 other fully accredited schools. "Why go to Podunk College," *Time* magazine asked, "when the Government will send you to Yale?"[6]

In February 1947 Benjamin Fine, education editor of the *New York Times* and director of a number of important postwar educational surveys, pointed out that although the colleges and universities were "crowded far beyond capacity, averaging a 50 per cent increase over their peacetime records," the teachers colleges had only "an enrollment of 150,000 compared with 143,000 in 1940." The teachers college enrollment, moreover, was misleading. A majority of the male students at these institutions had no desire to teach, and had enrolled there because no other school would accept them. Some veterans, contrary to their wishes and plans, suddenly found themselves at teachers colleges without even applying. Pennsylvania State College (now Pennsylvania State University), with more students than classroom space, farmed out two thousand of its freshmen to other state institutions, mainly teachers colleges. Similarly, the University of Minnesota assigned 2,500 of its freshmen to the School of Education for their first two years of college work, after which they could transfer to the liberal arts college.[7] In the fall of 1947 veterans constituted forty-nine percent of the total enrollment in higher education, but made up only thirty-nine

Table 2

EXPECTED AND CONFERRED DEGREES IN HIGHER EDUCATIONAL
INSTITUTIONS, 1940–1953

Academic Year	Expected Degrees†	Conferred Degrees*	Discrepancy‡
1939–1940	—	216,521	—
1940–1941	228,430	No data	—
1941–1942	240,339	213,491	−26,848
1942–1943	252,248	177,537 (est.)	−74,711
1943–1944	264,157	141,582	−122,575
1944–1945	276,066	149,466 (est.)	−126,600
1945–1946	287,975	157,349	−130,626
1946–1947	299,884	299,884 (est.)	—
1947–1948	311,793	317,607	+5,814
1948–1949	323,702	421,282	+97,580
1949–1950	335,611	496,874	+161,263
1950–1951	347,520	454,960	+107,440
1951–1952	359,429	401,203	+41,774
1952–1953	371,338	372,315	+977

Source: Historical Statistics of the United States, Colonial Times to 1957 (U.S. Bureau of the Census, 1960), p. 211.

†Based upon 5.5 percent average annual increase. Some comparative degree increases: 1920–1930 16.1 percent annual average; 1930–1940 5.5 percent; 1954–1964 7.2 percent.

‡I estimated the number of conferred degrees for 1942–1943 by dividing the differences between the 1942 and 1944 figures. I used the same method, only with 1944 and 1946 figures, to estimate the number of conferred degrees in 1944–1945. Had I utillized this method to estimate the number of conferred degrees in 1946–1947, I would have listed 237,478. Instead, I made a generous approximation.

percent of the students attending teachers colleges and thirty-eight percent of those registered at junior colleges.[8] This enrollment pattern existed throughout the veteran era.

Despite record enrollments and record numbers of degrees awarded (1940: 216,521; 1950: 496,661), the G.I. Bill seemingly failed to replenish the supply of college graduates lost to the war. The lack of adequate statistics, however, prevented a completely accurate determination of the number of degrees the war cost the nation. Until 1948 the U.S. Office of Education collected biennial rather than annual data. It provided no statistics, therefore, specifying the number of degrees awarded in 1943, 1945, and 1947. Nevertheless, assuming that institutions of higher learning continued during the 1940s the rate of average annual increase of degrees conferred during the 1930s and then plotting a chart (see Table 2) comparing anticipated degrees with earned degrees on a year-to-year basis, some conclusions emerge.[9] The nation lost 26,848 degrees in 1942; 122,575 in 1944; and 130,626 in 1946. By selecting numbers halfway between the figures for 1942 and 1944, and 1944 and 1946, it seems reasonable to suppose the nation lost an estimated 74,711 degrees in 1943 and 126,600 degrees in 1945. World War II, according to this logic, directly cost the nation 481,360 degrees between 1942 and 1946. In addition, unknown thousands of college graduates lost their lives during the war, pushing the total degree deficit well over the 500,000 mark. In thousands of instances, of course, the degree loss was temporary. By 1948 the number of degrees awarded exceeded the figure projected for that year, based on the above assumption, and by 1950 the gap between projected and conferred degrees reached 161,263. For the period 1948 to 1953, the nation's colleges granted 414,848 more degrees than normally would have been the case. They were not enough. As a rough summary estimate, the G.I. Bill veterans and the regular college students of the postwar years fell short by over 100,000 degrees to replenish the number of college graduates lost during World War II.

Some veterans would not or could not have attended college without the G.I. Bill. The V.A., however, made no survey and none of its application forms asked who among the G.I. Bill recipients had enrolled in college primarily because of the legislation. Two educators, Norman Frederiksen and William B. Schrader, on the other hand, devoted considerable effort to the subject. In an authoritative study they examined the college performance of 10,000 veteran and nonveteran students in sixteen carefully selected, representative American colleges. They concluded that "about ten per cent" of the veterans definitely would not have attended college without the G.I. Bill and that "another ten per cent would probably not have." [10] Of the 2,232,000 veterans who attended college under the G.I. Bill, therefore, only 446,400, or twenty percent, can be attributed directly to the legislation. In September 1950, to illustrate the Frederiksen-Schrader conclusion, 263,000 fewer veterans registered for the fall semester than had been enrolled during the spring semester. If all 263,000 failed to register because they had earned degrees, only 52,600, or twenty percent of the total, owed their diplomas solely to the G.I. Bill, the others supposedly would have earned degrees had there been no legislation and may best be called delayed or belated degrees. Put in another perspective, in 1950, the peak year of degrees, the veterans who could not or would not have gone to college without the G.I. Bill accounted for a relatively small fraction (9.4 percent) of all degrees (496,874 total degrees; 263,000 veteran degrees; 52,600 veteran degrees possible only with the G.I. Bill).

The Frederiksen-Schrader study, however thorough and professional, suffers from an insurmountable problem, the unreliability of human intentions. Generally the more difficult the task at hand, the wider the gap between original intention and completed performance. Eighty percent of the veterans may have believed, and perhaps still do believe, they would have gone to college without a G.I. Bill, but how many would have had the self-discipline to accept the reality of four years of college, part-time work, spartan living conditions, and increased indebtedness? What would have been the reaction of the nonveteran students toward ex-servicemen had the latter been a minority, rather than the majority of males on campus? Would an adverse reaction have discouraged veteran enrollment? And did the veteran stimulate or deter the high school senior's decision to enter college?

The difficulty of working with human intentions in a hypothetical situation, the lack of adequate statistics, and the immeasurable variables of the impact of war, prosperity, and rising expectations upon higher education make it impossible to conclude with precision or certitude about veteran enrollment under the G.I. Bill and its impact on higher education. The evidence strongly suggests, however, that the program failed to offset the degrees and enrollments lost to the war. It did enable 446,400 veterans to attend college and undoubtedly eased the financial burdens of the 1,785,600 veterans who earned delayed or belated degrees.

The unexpected numbers of veteran students helped generate a steady flow of writing about veterans and their educational experience. During the postwar years the very idea of sending former servicemen to college fascinated a large segment of the public, which lavished attention upon veterans. Everyone, it seemed, wanted to know how veterans felt about every facet of life and about every issue of the day. Educators, along with novelists, journalists, movie producers, editors, and others labored to discern and to generalize about veteran characteristics, activities, and problems. Veterans were good copy.

Several conditions stimulated scholarly studies. An educator interested in veteran adjustment and achievement could conduct an investigation without leaving his own campus. Veterans readily cooperated, as did the nonveterans needed by researchers for control groups. Records were accessible and officials friendly. Then too, everyone associated with higher education recognized that the veteran era was unique and soon would be over. Studying veterans also fulfilled a professional need, and it was enjoyable work. Educators documented and published the conclusions of their engaging work in hundreds of professional and semiprofessional journals and popular publications of all kinds.

Emphasizing their most important finding, educators consistently and emphatically agreed that the veterans who packed college classrooms were singularly mature. In article after article academicians ascribed to veterans traits generally associated with maturity. George A. Mac-Farland, professor and director of the Veterans' Advisory Council at the University of Pennsylvania, wrote, for example, that "the veteran is acknowledged to be serious, time conscious, industrious, and capable." University of Minnesota administrator, Curtis E. Avery, called veterans "assertive, positive, and active," while Professor Clifton L. Hall of George Peabody College for Teachers reported that veterans "contributed a steadying influence to college life." *Fortune* magazine, after a special study, concluded that the class of 1949 (seventy percent of whom were veterans) was "the best, . . . the most mature, . . . the most responsible, . . . and the most self-disciplined group" of college students in history. After "a survey of sixty typical colleges and universities," Benjamin Fine summarized that "almost everywhere" veterans "have brought to classrooms maturity and an attitude of serious motivation." An article in *Life* about G.I.'s at Harvard University concluded that "for seriousness, perceptiveness, steadiness, and all the other undergraduate virtues," the veteran students were "the best in Harvard's history." Harvard's president, James Conant, agreed. They were, he maintained, "the most mature and promising students Harvard has ever had." The favorable commentary about veteran maturity was overwhelming.[11]

The numerous descriptions and analyses of veteran maturity indicated that veterans generally made a rapid and satisfactory adjustment from a military to an academic role. Reports of calloused and cynical servicemen embittered by their war experiences were rare. Nevertheless, the adjustment of veterans remained for several years a subject of serious concern and continuing interest. Most veterans started college work with some trepidation. One study, covering veterans attending seven universities, listed the chief adjustment problems, in order of importance, as 1) learning to study and concentrate, 2) finances, 3) housing, 4) recall of old subject matter, and 5) being an older student, with learning to study twelve times more severe than being older.[12] In most cases, the widespread uneasiness quickly dissipated. The president of Stanford University, for example, made the typical observation that "the quickness and ease with which the veteran students adjusted to civilian life was very striking."[13] MacFarland, in his study at the University of Pennsylvania, concluded that "it was remarkable how quickly" veteran adjustment problems "settled down to a normal peace-time level." At the University of Texas forty-seven percent of the veterans of one study reported that they had required "about a month" to "get in the groove" of civilian life. This same study also concluded that "contrary to expectations, length of service is not positively correlated with difficulty of adjustment"; that "veterans whose college work was interrupted by military service had more trouble than those for whom this was not true"; and that "the same situation appears when those who had planned to enter college are compared with those who had made no such plans." This last conclusion directly contradicted earlier fears that the G.I. Bill would lure to college many ill-prepared and noncommitted veterans who in turn would become frustrated and disillusioned.[14]

Ease of adjustment to college and such traits as seriousness and responsibility were obvious signs of maturity, but these characteristics could not be evaluated precisely. Formal academic achievement, on the other hand, perhaps the most important index of maturity for college students, could be measured statistically, and in this area veterans surpassed the performances of their nonveteran classmates and set the tone of student scholarship for at least half a decade.

Educators quickly adopted a comparative method, with its control groups of veterans and nonveterans, to insure validity of their findings. The method, which could be applied to a single course for one semester or to a university for an entire year or to larger groups enrolled at a number of schools, attracted researchers and helped produce an impressive list of studies. These studies, however, varied greatly in sophistication. One group merely compared the grade-point average of veterans and nonveterans within a specific administrative unit. During the spring and fall semesters of 1946, Byron H. Atkinson, coordinator of special student services at U.C.L.A., for example," selected at random" approximately 1,500 veteran and 1,500 nonveteran undergraduates (totaling over twenty-five percent of the school's undergraduates) and grouped them according to major fields of study. After comparing grades, Atkinson concluded that veteran performance was "appreciably higher in all groups and in all semesters, with the exception of Group I in the Fall Semester." Following their study of 2,000 veterans and 5,887 nonveterans at Ohio State University during the winter quarter of 1946, Ronald B. Thompson and Marie A. Flesher reported the veterans "showed about seven per cent more records of B or better, and the same per cent fewer below the grade required for graduation," and a "slightly superior" overall academic average. During the early autumn of 1947, Benjamin Fine toured campuses throughout the East and Middle West and found college presidents and professors impressed by the "maturity and eagerness and . . . better than average grades" of veterans. "The G.I.'s," Fine wrote, "are hogging the honor rolls and the Dean's lists." *Newsweek* pointed out that not one of Columbia University's 7,826 veterans "was in serious scholastic difficulty at the last marking period." During the spring semester of 1947 only thirty-five of the 6,010 veterans at the University of Minnesota suffered academic dismissal, about one-half of one percent compared to the normal civilian rate of over ten percent. At Hobart College four civilians flunked out for each veteran.[15]

Veterans, by failing less and earning higher grades, raised the level of work at most schools. "They study so hard," one Lehigh sophomore (nonveteran) complained, "we have to slave to keep up with them." [16] Nonveterans at Stanford University called veterans D.A.R.'s, for "Damn Average Raisers." The studies overwhelmingly documented the superior academic achievement of veterans and removed all doubt about the feasibility and desirability of paying veterans to attend college.[17] Educators who compiled and published these comparative studies often indicated that their findings countered critics who earlier had warned against "the development of public 'parasites.' " [18] Yale University President Charles Seymour commented about the "surprisingly" few failures and high percentages of honor students among the veterans. In his study, Fine remarked that veteran superiority came "much to the surprise of the skeptics who thought the veterans were . . . an educational problem." [19]

A second group of studies moved beyond a literal comparison of veteran and nonveteran grades and attempted to hold constant several variables before embarking upon comparative examinations. For a doctoral dissertation at Iowa State University, Arthur M. Gowan studied veterans and nonveterans and found a "highly significant" veteran academic superiority. He considered this familiar conclusion especially meaningful because he "noted that the mean high-school average and the mean A.C.E. [the psychological examination prepared by the American Council on Education] score for the non-veterans exceeded that of the veterans." At Northwestern University Edward L. Clark matched veterans and nonveterans of five component colleges according to ability (determined by scholastic-aptitude test scores) and found that veterans earned "slightly, though significantly better grades" despite "certain items of educational history presaging lower college records." In their study of freshmen who entered the College of Liberal Arts at the State University of Iowa in September 1946, Jean M. Crose and Norman W. Garmezy equated veterans and non-veterans according to "sex, marital status, race, academic classification, and composite entrance examination percentile rank." Veterans, they subsequently summarized, maintained a small but measurable academic superiority over nonveterans.[20]

Another group of studies that advanced beyond comparison of grades examined the performance of men whose military service had interrupted their college careers. Although differing in the number of records examined, the major programs veterans pursued, and the colleges selected for examination, almost all studies revealed that collectively veterans who attended college before entering service raised their grades when they returned to college.[21] In many cases the individual veterans studied had been in academic difficulty before the war and many others had records that indicated marginal chances of rehabilitation. The investigations distinctly implied that military service or age led to improved academic work. Two factors, however, temper this implication. First, the veterans who resumed their broken college education probably represented a more serious, more motivated group than the veterans who failed to do so. And second, only two studies considered the tendency of most students in general to improve their grades as they advanced from freshman to senior status.[22]

By far the most sophisticated of all studies of college-enrolled veterans was the Frederiksen-Schrader study financed by the Carnegie Foundation for the Advancement of Teaching and based on an elaborate questionnaire administered to 10,000 students during the spring semester of 1946–1947. As three primary objectives, Frederiksen and Schrader intended to find the answers to these questions:

1) Do veteran students make better grades in college, in relation to their ability, than nonveteran students?
2) What light does information about background, attitudes, and other qualities throw upon veteran-nonveteran differences?
3) How do veterans who could not have attended college without the financial assistance provided through the G.I. Bill compare with veteran students who were financially able to attend college?

Frederiksen and Schrader assembled twenty-five groups of students containing both veterans and nonveterans. The groups were as homogeneous as possible with respect to scholastic ability and aptitude, college program, "previous college training as a civilian, and educational environment while in college." Twenty of these groups contained veterans who had not entered college before their military service.

In these groups veterans earned grades superior to those of nonveterans of the same ability in sixteen instances. In each of the five groups that compared veterans with interrupted education with nonveterans whose education had not been interrupted, the veterans earned higher grades and showed "a marked gain" over their own prewar performances. In general, Frederiksen and Schrader found that despite superior grades, veterans "tended to ascribe slightly" less importance to grades than did the nonveterans. This part of the Frederiksen-Schrader study, devoted to the comparison of veteran and nonveteran academic achievement, confirmed what smaller, less ambitious studies already had indicated: that veterans, overwhelmingly but not universally, did better college work relative to their ability than nonveterans. The difference in grades usually ranged from a fourth to a third of a letter grade.[23]

Frederiksen and Schrader also tried to find out why veterans were better students. With sound quantitative methods, they compared the following background characteristics: father's education, father's income, size of home community, secondary school, opinion of preparation for college, work experience, and college living quarters. The results of the investigation, while providing considerable information about the backgrounds of college students in the spring of 1947, offered no help or insight to account for veteran superiority. Nonveterans and veterans differed in certain characteristics (fathers of nonveterans, for example, generally had more formal education than fathers of veterans) but the differences could not be related with any validity to academic achievement. In fact, the study concluded that when the two groups of students were "alike with respect to these characteristics," there would be no noticeable change in college performance.[24]

Frederiksen and Schrader also examined factors related to motivation in order to explain veteran superiority. They collected, tabulated, analyzed, and compared veteran and nonveteran replies to questions about the reasons for going to college, vocational plans, intentions to accelerate programs, and adjustments to demands of college. Although there were differences in some aspects of academic motivation between the two groups, the superiority of veterans could not "be explained on the basis" of these differences.[25] Nor did a comparative study of veteran and nonveteran utilization of time (for classes, studying, athletics, bull sessions, paid employment, and unrequired academic pursuits) yield results that accounted for higher veteran grades. This survey of how students spent their time reported only "slight" differences between the amount of time veterans and nonveterans devoted to any of the above activities. Both categories of students also expressed "quite similar attitudes toward their college and its program." In general background, motivation, disposition of time, and view of college Frederiksen and Schrader found no significant difference between veteran and nonveteran students.[26]

In one important area, however, veterans were different; they were older. But after investigation, Frederiksen and Schrader concluded that "the question as to whether or not the superiority of veteran students is merely a function of greater age cannot be rigorously answered." Their findings suggested "that greater age, in and of itself, can not account for veteran-nonveteran difference" in academic achievement. When they eliminated the oldest group of veterans from their samples, it "virtually" destroyed "any correlation" between age and grades among the veterans and left the remaining " 'younger' veteran group superior by a substantial (though reduced) amount to the nonveteran group." The failure to establish age as the reason veterans excelled in college left that question unanswered.[27]

Frederiksen and Schrader, as noted in their primary objectives, wanted to move beyond a comparison of veterans and nonveterans to examine the similarities and variations of background, characteristics, and achievements among veterans. Accordingly, they found "the typical veteran believed . . . that his service experience made him more eager to go to college," and that the experience had not lessened his scholastic ability.[28] Since the great majority of veterans had received no college training (in such programs as the navy's V-12) and had not taken college-level correspondence courses, their tendency to earn grades higher than those of nonveterans cannot be attributed to training gained while in service. In fact, veterans who had received some college-level training while in uniform did not earn significantly higher grades than those veterans without this experience. There were, furthermore, "slight tendencies" for greater achievement, relative to ability, "to be associated with greater length of service and higher rank." Also, veterans who never left the United States generally surpassed the academic achievement of those veterans who served overseas. By its negative findings, that no correlation existed between academic accomplishment and overseas travel (with or without combat) or college-level service training, the Frederiksen-Schrader study dispelled two widely held opinions about why veterans excelled as students. The study's positive findings, that the best students were veterans who had been away from school the longest, who were married, and who were older, contradicted the dominant expectation of veteran performance.[29]

To persons committed to expanding educational opportunities, the most important Frederiksen-Schrader investigation compared the differences between veterans who would have gone to college even without a G.I. Bill to those veterans who would not have gone without the program. The typical veteran in the latter group "was older, had been out of school longer, had served longer, had been overseas longer, came from a family with less educational background, was more likely to be married, and was probably less likely to be planning to enter a profession than were the other veterans." Despite these differences, there was no "consistent difference in *ability* level" between the two groups. But in performance, the veterans who would not have gone to college without the G.I. Bill "earned slightly better grades relative to ability than did those who probably would have attended in any case." [30]

Veterans were a heterogeneous group, as the Frederiksen-Schrader examination of grades and backgrounds illustrated. The identification of subgroups among veteran students led Frederiksen and Schrader to draw a hypothesis that explained why veterans were better students than nonveterans and why some groups of veterans surpassed other groups in achievement. "The superiority of the veteran student," they hypothesized, "was not due primarily to any psychological characteristics associated with greater age or with experience connected with military service." Instead, they declared it "was due to a process of self-selection growing out of a complex of circumstances which included the educational benefits of the G.I. Bill and the delaying of college matriculation on the part of veterans. Those veterans who decided to go to college included a larger *proportion* of strongly motivated and academically-minded men than would otherwise have gone to college." [31]

This hypothesis frustrates the historian. Frederiksen and Schrader rightfully and readily admitted that individual decisions grow from "a complex of circumstances," which in reality present insurmountable problems for the historian. To illustrate: One Iowa farm boy took his G.I. Bill and went to college, while another did not. From the letters their mothers and girl friends saved, the historian may learn that one liked animals, the outdoors, and being his own boss, so wanted to stay on the farm. The other veteran, meanwhile, eagerly registered at the state university to study chemistry, a subject which had fascinated him since boyhood when an uncle surprised him with a gift chemistry set. Such letters, however acceptable as sources, do not tell the historian much beyond one particular veteran's greater desire for academic study. With sufficient training, time, and the cooperation of the two veterans, the historian might learn what experience or series of experiences shaped their personalities. It would be impossible, of course, for historians to pursue meaningful investigations with a sufficient number of veterans (both those who went to college and those who did not) in order to establish certain patterns. Historians instead must be content with the simple, obvious generalization that veterans who attended college were, as a group, more highly motivated than other students.

Like the G.I. Bill itself, the veterans of World War II can be understood only in the context of their times. Looking back a quarter of a century later few persons are surprised that young men who, for the most part, were teenagers during the nation's greatest economic depression and who took part in a world war, both rather sobering experiences, proved to be serious, highly motivated college students. Before 1946, however, the public had a different, less generous estimation of the veteran-student. Sending able-bodied veterans to college was a new idea and as a new idea carried an inevitable degree of uncertainty, producing an element of fear. Many veterans, critics pointed out, would be poor students and would drink more and have different attitudes toward sex than would traditional college students. And the general picture of the veteran, based upon the experiences of the 1920s and 1930s, was even worse. The apprehensions, of course, proved ill founded. The academic achievement of the veterans who went to college countered the public's anxiety and created instead a favorable image of the veteran. In a postwar era filled with disappointment, the record enrollment and academic achievement of the veterans who went to college under the G.I. Bill must be considered one of the country's pleasant surprises.

4. Administration

The veterans' training program at the college level has enjoyed more harmony and success than any other phase of the program. . . . Considered as a whole, there is little question that better training was received at the college level for less money than in any other phase of the veterans' training program.

Report of the House Select Committee To Investigate
Educational Program under G.I. Bill, February 1952.

Compared with the other types of training pursued by veterans, the program at the college level has operated more satisfactorily. The problems involved were less serious, largely because the institutions were better equipped than other schools and industries to meet immediately the needs of the new, adult students.

Report of the President's Commission on Veterans'
Pensions, September 1956.

IN THEORY and operation the G.I. Bill's college program combined an uneven mixture of federal, state, institutional, and individual responsibility and cooperation. The veteran enjoyed complete freedom to select the education he wished, but he had to attend an institution approved by the state in which the school was located. While the Veterans' Administration certified entitlement and authorized payments, full control of the veteran's education rested with the institution. Congress, meanwhile, could and did modify the program through its legislative actions. Each administrative unit, the V.A., Congress, state governments, colleges, and veterans, had its particular characteristics, problems, and history. Together, however, they ran a program distinguished for its magnitude and its success. Close to two and a quarter million veterans attended approximately 2,000 institutions of higher learning at a cost of about five and a half billion dollars.

Following passage of the G.I. Bill in June 1944, the V.A. combined the educational provisions of the act with the existing rehabilitation program under the direction of the assistant administrator for pensions and compensation. When the V.A. reorganized itself in 1946 to adjust to the growing demands on its services, it created a separate Vocational Rehabilitation and Education division, headed by an assistant administrator. As part of the reorganization the V.A. established thirteen branch offices, with a vocational rehabilitation and education director in each, and delegated to them full responsibility for the operation of the G.I. Bill's programs. Below the thirteen branch offices in the organizational chart were the sixty-nine regional offices which continued to perform, through their education sections, tasks associated with running the college program. Meanwhile, the central office in Washington functioned as the policy-making and supervising body.

The V.A. administrative organization looked better on paper than it did in operation. Congress continually pressured for reductions in staff and facilities within the Vocational Rehabilitation and Education division. During fiscal 1947 and 1948, for example, it sharply reduced the division's appropriations at the peak of the division's work load. After the V.A. abolished the branch offices in 1949, the regional offices constantly referred decisions to the central office, at a certain cost in efficiency. Even when the V.A. had funds, it could not always find, hire, and train the number of persons it needed to administer its programs. During the first four months of 1946, the Vocational Rehabilitation and Education division payroll jumped from 8,390 to 21,803 employees. In 1951, a House select committee reported that "through all echelons of the Veterans' Administration framework, [the committee] found personnel lacking the education and experience necessary to qualify them as administrators of an educational program." [1] Little wonder that veterans and colleges sometimes received their checks months late or that inquiries often received unsatisfactory replies. Had the V.A. improved its public relations, another weakness, it may have convinced Congress to provide the money and authority it needed. [2]

While any agency would have encountered problems administering a program with the dimensions of the G.I. Bill, the V.A. could have helped itself by developing a meaningful relationship with the educational community in general and with the United States Office of Education in particular. The U.S. Commissioner of Education, Earl J. McGrath, insisted in 1952 that his office "had no direct or indirect share in administering the Servicemen's Readjustment Act." A year earlier a House select committee reported that there was "little evidence which indicates that the Veterans' Administration sought the advice and assistance of established educational groups in organizing the vocational rehabilitation and education service and establishing its policy." Five years later the President's Commission on Veterans' Pensions, repeating the same theme, concluded that "perhaps the greatest weakness in the administration of the program under Public Law 346 was the apparent lack of interest or inability on the part of the V.A. in developing sound working relationships with the States and with private educational institutions." Perhaps the principal result of this failure was the less generous provisions of the subsequent Korean G.I. Bill. [3]

The Servicemen's Readjustment Act of 1944 authorized the administrator of the V.A. to "prescribe and promulgate such rules and regulations as may be necessary to carry out its purposes and provisions." For the college program to operate the V.A. had to establish rules and regulations in a number of areas. Until the amendment to the act in December 1945 eliminated the age limitation, the V.A. had to decide whether to accept or reject a veteran's petition that, although he was over twenty-five years old when he entered service, the war had interrupted his education. Since the law failed to define "ordinary school year" or what constituted a "full-time" course, the V.A. had to prescribe definitions and apportion corresponding subsistence payments. [4] It also developed a payment schedule for veterans taking correspondence courses and ruled what was a "fair and reasonable" tuition for each school selecting that method of tuition payment. Although the law provided a student-veteran with a leave not exceeding thirty days per calendar year while attending school, the V.A. established when and under what circumstances the veteran took his leave. In December 1945 the V.A. decided to add ten percent handling charge to supply and book vouchers that colleges submitted for payment, a practice that the V.A. extended less often to institutions offering below college-level instruction.

When the V.A. acted to interpret and administer the G.I. Bill, its decisions and policies were consistently generous toward veterans and colleges, although a few colleges might have argued differently after a disagreement over tuition. Without exception, the V.A. accepted as valid every veteran's claim that the war had interrupted his education. Following its survey (1950–1951) of education under the G.I. Bill, the General Accounting Office concluded that the V.A.'s liberal "interpretation of the law covering leave added over $41,000,000 to the cost of subsistence payments to college students." As long as a veteran had sufficient days of entitlement for educational benefits for the first half of a semester the V.A. paid his tuition, fees, books, and subsistence for the entire semester. And if a veteran, as he approached the exhaustion of his entitlement, realized he lacked days to reach the semester's halfway mark, the V.A. permitted him to buy back leave days and thus add sufficiently to his entitlement to gain the bonus. To relieve the strain on the working capital of colleges the V.A. paid tuition on a monthly basis rather than at the completion of a semester or quarter. In May 1947 Dr. Francis J. Brown, representing the American Council on Education at a Senate hearing, praised the V.A. for its liberal interpretations. He added, moreover, that Harold V. Stirling, the V.A. official whose division administered the G.I. Bill, "has said, not once but many times before our committee, if the law permitted it he would like to see the V.A. pay all the costs of education of the veteran." [5]

The V.A.'s eagerness to exercise as generous and as complete a role as possible in the administration of the G.I. Bill also became evident in its guidance and counseling program. Since everyone connected with the writing of the act wanted to avoid any semblance of federal dictation to the veteran as to his course of study, the act permitted but did not require the V.A. to provide counseling and guidance to the veteran. But almost from the beginning, and with the blessing of the American Council on Education, the V.A. moved to develop a counseling program. The task was not hard because the law that provided rehabilitation and training for disabled veterans included mandatory vocational counseling. Starting in June 1944, therefore, at the City College of New York the V.A. established a series of centers (382 in existence in May 1947) across the country. It required disabled veterans to use these centers, and it encouraged the able-bodied veterans to do the same.[6] Over ninety percent of the centers were associated with a college or university and all operated under a contractual arrangement with the V.A. As a rough estimate, over a million G.I. Bill college students received guidance from these centers. All the studies evaluating this massive program agreed that generally it was a success. Veterans who used this service, for example, had a lower dropout rate than the veterans who failed to take advantage of free testing and guidance.[7] Although the V.A. readily and successfully established a guidance and counseling program, it just as willingly curtailed its program when veteran enrollment dropped and colleges accelerated their own counseling programs.

The V.A.'s major operational problem with the college program concerned tuition charges, mainly at publicly controlled schools with traditionally low tuition. The G.I. Bill specified that the V.A. would pay institutions up to $500 per year for tuition, fees, books, and supplies. If a college charged no tuition or a tuition that did not cover the actual cost of educating a student, the V.A. could determine and pay a "fair and reasonable compensation," within the $500 limit.[8] Actually the V.A., within its legislative authority, could and did offer colleges a choice of four tuition plans: it paid customary charges; it paid, as a minimum figure, $15 per month, $45 per quarter, and $60 per semester; it paid the nonresident tuition rate for all veterans at public institutions; and it paid tuition based on the estimated cost of instruction. Problems developed, especially between the V.A. and the colleges that selected the last option of tuition payment. Some municipal and state schools chose this plan because by law they could not charge tuition to residents.[9] Too often the V.A. and public colleges that preferred this method of payment disagreed about what constituted a "fair and reasonable compensation" for educating a veteran. Some public institutions that selected the option of collecting nonresident tuition for all its veterans clearly raised the rates beyond the actual cost of instruction.[10] Other colleges, when they calculated the cost of instruction, included as expense the salaries of professors paid from federal funds, and therefore not legitimately an expense. And some colleges failed to notify the V.A. when a veteran registered but did not attend classes. To deal with tuition problems the administrator of the V.A. relied upon an advisory committee of four (later increased to thirteen) leading educators he recruited in 1944. The difficulties involved with college tuition

Registration at the University of Denver, 1946.

National Archives

Quonset huts used as classroom buildings at the University
of Kentucky, 1947.

University of Kentucky University and Educational Archives

At the University of Wisconsin, 1947.

State Historical Society of Wisconsin

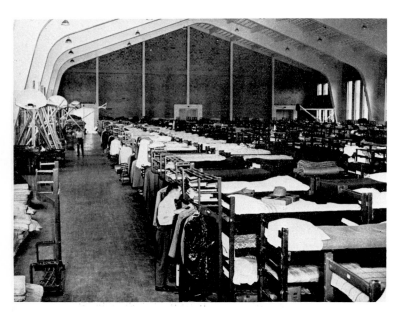

Barracks for single veterans at the University of Maryland.

University of Maryland Photo Archives

Prefabricated housing units being placed at the University of Kentucky.

University of Kentucky University and Educational Archives

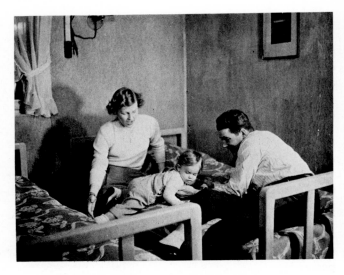

A student veteran and his family at home in veterans' housing at the University of Kentucky.

University of Kentucky
University and Educational Archives

Housing for married veterans at the University of Wisconsin.

University Extension, University of Wisconsin

payments under the G.I. Bill did not stem from administrative policy decisions nor statutory limits, but from the small minority of college administrators who took advantage of the program to advance their institutions' financial positions and from the honest difficulty the V.A. and the colleges had agreeing on a definition of "fair and reasonable." [11]

A second category of problems that accompanied the operation of the G.I. Bill's college program dealt with books, supplies, and equipment. Within the $500 limit for tuition, fees, and supplies, the V.A. paid each veteran's bill for the books and incidentals needed to take a course. In most cases, a veteran went to his campus bookstore, picked out the books and supplies needed, signed his name, and left. The bookstore collected the veteran's bill, plus ten percent for handling charges, from the V.A. Often, however, the handling charges pushed the cost of educating the veteran over the statutory boundary of $500 per year per student. Petty graft thrived. Bookstores that sold books at an across-the-board discount, charged veterans full list price. Some stores charged a flat rate for minor supplies regardless of the amount involved and maintained no record of the items issued to the veteran. Professors approved veterans' requests to obtain equipment for use in a course although the equipment, though useful, was not required. Countless veterans ordered a loose-leaf notebook for every course and a fountain pen and dictionary once a semester. Veterans could defend a brief case as a needed supply and English and history majors easily justified a typewriter for their term papers. The abuse came when some veterans made the same justification semester after semester.[12] In actual dollars or percentage of the program's total cost, the amount of money lost through this petty graft was minor. Although only a tiny fraction of all veterans abused the book and supplies allowance, their distribution throughout the country tarnished the image of this portion of the program.

The G.I. Bill college program did experience operational problems, but on balance they were minor. The most severe problem, tuition, involved in controversy only about twenty million, or about one percent of the two billion paid in college tuition. During the 1950s the V.A., the General Accounting Office, a House Select Committee, and a President's Commission all investigated the G.I. Bill's entire educational program and implicitly or explicitly arrived at the same broad conclusion that "the veterans' training program at the college level . . . enjoyed more harmony and success than any other phase of the program"; and the college program offered better training "for less money than [did] . . . any other phase of the veterans' training program." [13] On the other hand, graft, waste, and inefficiency in varying degrees characterized on-the-job training, institutional on-farm training, and training below the college level. The reasons for the superiority of the college program were obvious. The colleges offered established curriculums of proven value, already operated the needed administrative structure, and required little supervision. And, of course, the veterans at the college level were the brightest and best educated of all the former servicemen who improved their training under the G.I. Bill. All this did not mean that the G.I. Bill's college program functioned smoothly on the nation's campuses. It did not, because there were too many veterans for existing facilities.

Congress, while not involved with the day-to-day operation of the G.I. Bill, exercised its power and influence in several ways. Because the measure did not invest the V.A. with authority to supervise education and it did not spell out procedural guidelines of administration, the result sometimes was inefficiency, graft, and waste. To help check these weaknesses Congress first investigated and analyzed how various parts of the G.I. Bill worked, and then passed a series of restrictive amendments to the original act. Starting in 1945 and continuing to 1950, it established standards for agricultural training, vocational schools, and on-the-job training; provided funds to the states to intensify their supervision of training facilities; and granted the V.A. power to deny approval to schools at all levels that were less than a year old. And in August 1949 it created a Veterans Tuition Appeals Board, whose decisions were final.[14]

Although Congress modified the interests and programs of thousands of veteran students with each of these amendments, it altered the income, and presumably the living standard, of every veteran student when it increased the subsistence allowance, effective 1 April 1948. The increases Congress voted in December 1945 (from $50 to $65 for single and from $75 to $90 for married veterans) reflected the inflationary rise in the nation's economy during the eighteen months between passage of the G.I. Bill and December 1945. When the cost of living continued to climb throughout 1946, 1947, and 1948, it was natural that the veteran demand for a second subsistence increase grew accordingly.

Starting in the summer of 1946, magazines and newspapers reported survey findings that very few veterans could live on their subsistence checks.[15] Throughout 1947, with chapters of the American Veterans Committee spearheading the movement, veterans on campuses in the Northeast, Midwest, and Far West flooded President Truman and

Congress with statistics supporting their petitions for more money. The petitions showed, for example, that the cost of living had risen eighteen percent during 1946. By January 1948 the AVC's "Operation Subsistence" claimed one million supporters.[16] Congress responded. The House conducted hearings during February, March, April, and May 1947, and the Senate did the same in May and June 1947. Acting upon their committees' recommendations, the Senate passed a bill in July 1947, and the House in February 1948, raising the subsistence allowance to $75 for single, $105 for veterans with one dependent, and $120 for veterans with two or more dependents. The slower action in the House resulted from the influence of Mississippi's John E. Rankin, chairman of the House Committee on Veterans' Affairs, and from the positions of the American Legion and the American Council on Education. Rankin did not want subsistence checks to compete with wages in the South. In the spring of 1947, the Legion wanted more time for investigation before taking a position, and the American Council on Education, after making a nationwide study, recommended no increase except to inaugurate a monthly $10 payment for the first child and $7.50 for each additional child.[17]

The debate about increased subsistence payments reopened discussion on the intent of the original act with regard to these payments. Florida's Senator Claude Pepper, author of one of the several bills to increase the monthly allowances, argued that "I was a member of this committee [Subcommittee on Labor and Public Welfare] when this bill [Servicemen's Readjustment Act of 1944] was reported out, and I was there when it was considered. . . . As to the intent of Congress. . . . we never expected that the amount we determined upon would be less than the amount required to maintain decent living for the beneficiary." Dr. Francis J. Brown concluded just the opposite. He reported that he too had "sat through all of the hearings while the original bill and its amendments were under consideration" and that both he and the ACE clearly understood the intent of the act was to assist, "not . . . provide free education for every veteran." Both positions, of course, had supporters, but Congress refrained from making any clarifying statement regarding the intent of the subsistence allowance.[18]

In addition to amending the G.I. Bill, Congress directly shaped the operation of the college program by establishing two projects that supplied colleges with desperately needed buildings. These projects eased the pressure on the colleges' inadequate physical plants and made possible the additional enrollment of perhaps 400,000 veterans.

As usual, the conditions on the nation's campuses merely reflected the conditions within society as a whole. Between 1945 and 1950 the United States suffered the most acute housing shortage in its history, the aftermath of a decade and a half of depression and war. At one time Chicago reported 100,000 homeless veterans, while in Atlanta 2,000 persons responded to a single advertisement of a vacancy. Millions of American families lived in hastily remodeled attics, garages, basements, barns, and other substandard housing, or else "doubled up" with relatives or friends. As early as January 1945 a nationwide survey by the *New York Times* reported that colleges were "turning away thousands of discharged war veterans because of insufficient housing, overcrowded classrooms and lack of instructional staff." The most serious shortage, the survey continued, was housing, especially for the married veterans. Sixteen months later Robert M. Hutchins, president of the University of Chicago, aptly declared that "the crisis in education about which the country is now hearing is a housing crisis." [19]

In June 1945, two months before Japan surrendered, Congress took its first step to combat veteran dissatisfaction with the housing shortage. It amended the Lanham Act of 1940, which authorized the federal government to construct public housing in connection with defense and the war effort. According to the amendment the National Housing Administration could rent existing defense or war housing to veterans and could construct additional temporary housing units. If colleges were willing to move buildings to their campuses, they could obtain them without charge. Six months later Congress again amended the Lanham Act to accelerate the Veterans Reuse Program. The new amendment authorized funds to pay the costs of moving and converting housing units into veteran student housing and to reimburse colleges that already had incurred such expenses. Within six weeks the applications for this housing exceeded three times the available units. Congress responded by appropriating $253,727,000, in addition to the original $191,900,000, to keep the program operating. When the funds ran out in August 1946, the Federal Public Housing Administration reported that it had allocated to the nation's colleges 101,462 accommodations, consisting of 51,761 family dwellings and 49,701 dormitory types. At their own expense, but under authority of the Reuse Program, colleges transferred buildings that housed another 38,160 students. Typical transfers under the program included nine surplus naval barracks, each capable of housing twenty veteran families, from Newport, Rhode Island, to the Massachusetts Institute of Technology and thirty-nine portable duplex houses from the Willow Run defense complex to the University of Michigan.[20]

To supplement the Reuse Program, colleges gained approximately 100,000 accommodations for veterans through the use of surplus federal structures within commuting distance of their campuses. Stanford University, for example, acquired the use of Dibble General Hospital; the University of New Mexico utilized former bachelor officers quarters at nearby Kirtland Field; Rutgers University used barracks buildings at Camp Kilmer; and Hiram College took over apartments at the Ravenna Ordnance Plant.[21] Colleges also gained 33,260 campus housing accommodations through the Temporary Education Facilities for Veterans program and indeterminable off-campus accommodations at public war housing projects under management of the Federal Public Housing Administration or under various city, county, or state governments, which by law gave preference to veterans. At peak enrollment, perhaps as many as 300,000 veterans resided in housing provided under the amendments to the Lanham Act.[22] Considering that thousands of veterans accelerated their educational programs while others attended college only to complete a degree the war interrupted or to obtain a masters degree, the total number of student veterans who at sometime lived in this temporary housing was appreciably higher.

But colleges also needed buildings other than housing if they were to increase enrollment to meet veteran demand. Early in 1946 the American Council on Education reported widespread shortages of college classrooms, libraries, administration buildings, cafeterias, student unions, and other structures that constitute a college's physical plant. Various colleges, education associations, and veteran organizations reported the same situation and turned to Congress for assistance. In August Congress took the logical and popular action and again amended the Lanham Act, this time to use surplus war buildings "to provide needed educational facilities, other than housing, to educational institutions furnishing courses of training or education to persons under title II of the Servicemen's Readjustment Act of 1944, as amended."[23]

The new law empowered the Federal Works Agency to transfer surplus military buildings to any educational institution where the United States Office of Education found an acute shortage of floor space.[24] Called the Veterans' Educational Facilities Program, the legislation required a college to furnish a prepared site and to install the utilities, while the federal government financed the disassembly, transportation, and reerection of the buildings, complete with needed remodeling and equipment. Congress appropriated a total of $79,130,000 for the operation of the transfers, plus $4,000,000 for administrative expenses. In June 1948 workmen moved the last of 5,920 used, temporary structures providing 18,375,196 square feet of floor space.[25] More than 700 colleges benefited. Under the V.E.F.P., parts of the powder experimental laboratory at the Susquehanna Ordnance Depot in Pennsylvania accommodated students on five separate campuses, while a barracks at Fort Washington, Maryland, became a classroom and faculty office building at Juniata College. Meanwhile, the University of California at Berkeley received seventeen buildings totaling 185,800 square feet of floor space, including an armory and a cafeteria. Impressive as the program was, the buildings supplied only seventy-eight percent of the space the United States Office of Education judged colleges urgently needed and fifty-one percent of the capacity classified justifiably needed.

Two other provisions of the V.E.F.P. helped the colleges. Under the first, colleges could obtain without cost a wide range of surplus property from various federal agencies. Before the program terminated on 31 December 1948, colleges obtained, at less than cost, $114,041,000 worth of equipment including classroom furniture, books, motor vehicles, lockers, air conditioners, chemical and medical supplies, and electronics equipment. Under the second provision, colleges could purchase in advance of public sales and at a price representing a tiny fraction of the real value a host of items, such as equipment for infirmaries, cafeterias and laboratories. The purchase program operated from 6 October 1946 to 31 March 1947, during which time colleges acquired property valued at $9,956,000.[26]

The contribution of state governments toward the operation of the G.I. Bill's college program involved, in essence, greater appropriations to public colleges within their borders. In this respect the states continued during 1945 to 1950 their traditional marked spending differences.

Of all the states, New York faced the greatest challenge to accommodate the higher education demands of veterans. It contained approximately ten percent of the country's population and therefore had a proportionately larger problem. Equally important, after 1945, when New Jersey transformed Rutgers University into a state university, New York was the only state without a public university. In addition, each year the number of high school graduates leaving the state for their college training exceeded the number entering from other states. During 1941–1942, for example, the difference was 14,000 students, a total greater than the enrollment at all but a handful of the nation's universities.

New York State traditionally relied upon private colleges and universities to educate its youth, thereby annually driving thousands of high school graduates to low-tuition state universities in other parts of the country. In lieu of a state university, New York maintained within an unwieldy administrative structure: the forestry college at Syracuse University; the agriculture, veterinary science, industrial and labor relations, and home economics programs at Cornell University; the ceramics department at Alfred University; eleven teachers colleges; and numerous two-year technical and agricultural institutions. A new Yorker desirous of a degree in the liberal arts, engineering, law, journalism, or fine arts had to enroll at a private school.[27]

The educational situation following World War II brought the New York State structure to a crisis position. With the government paying their tuition, veterans around the country flocked to the state's prestigious private schools, such as Columbia, Rensselaer Polytechnic Institute, Cornell, and Rochester. Enrollment demands in other states forced one state university after another to ban nonresidents, even veteran nonresidents. Meanwhile, the assorted New York state schools, with their severely limited offerings, attracted proportionately few veterans. In November 1946 the enrollment at the teachers colleges stood thirty-two percent higher than the enrollment of October 1941, but during the same period the enrollments at the private institutions soared: Rochester, 73 percent; Syracuse 111 percent; and R.P.I. 132 percent. While seven of the teachers colleges still had not reached their established capacity, the private schools far exceeded theirs.[28]

The state education department and Governor Thomas E. Dewey had anticipated higher enrollments, but the magnitude of the increase during the early weeks of 1946 climbed far beyond expectations and forced Dewey to act. He called a meeting for 7 and 8 March of the presidents of the state's private colleges and universities and outlined an emergency state program. Since the existing campuses, even with maximum expansion, could not accommodate all the veterans, Dewey reasoned that the state should open several temporary colleges, particularly one at the large Sampson Naval Training base near Geneva, New York.[29] Since the war's end educators had eyed covetously the buildings on numerous military installations around the state and therefore readily accepted Dewey's proposal.

There were other factors promoting a quick acceptance of Dewey's plan. Dewey and the presidents of private colleges realized that failure to accommodate all qualified veterans who sought a higher education would be politically dangerous. Two weeks before Dewey set the date for the conference of presidents, the Democratic Party leadership introduced bills in the state legislature authorizing creation of a state university at a cost of fifty million dollars. This demand for a state university followed a release by the New York City Mayor's Committee on Unity, which documented college discrimination in the city and state against Jews, Catholics, and Negroes. By backing the idea of several temporary state campuses (with no discriminatory admission standards), the private college presidents could argue that there was no need for a permanent state university. Equally important, the presidents, by their cooperation, could help shape and direct the entire project and thereby better block any attempt to establish a state university. In a letter to George D. Stoddard, New York State Commissioner of Education, Chancellor William P. Tolley of Syracuse University candidly wrote that "we do not want an embryo of a state university at Sampson." The way to avoid it, Tolley suggested, "would be the operation at Sampson under a joint board composed of representatives of Syracuse, Cornell, Colgate, Hobart, and possibly Rochester." [30] Stoddard, Dewey, and the presidents of these private institutions agreed with Tolley's sentiments. Dewey's plan also meant that the private colleges would face less retrenchment when the veteran enrollment subsided.

Dewey, the state, and the college presidents moved quickly. On 17 May 1946 the state issued a temporary charter to the Associated Colleges of Upper New York (ACUNY) establishing a board of trustees to oversee three campuses. All of the trustees were college presidents of private schools in the state. The state assumed all financial responsibility and the federal government, through the amended Lanham Act, provided the physical plant and equipment. Four months later Governor Dewey officially opened Champlain College, housed in the brick and limestone buildings of the Plattsburg Barracks, a 727-acre campuslike military base dating back to 1814. Bordering on scenic Lake Champlain, twenty miles south of the Canadian border, the college had an instant enrollment of 1,101 students, ninety percent veterans and ninety-nine percent male. Within a month ACUNY opened a 175-acre campus on the grounds and in the temporary buildings of the army's Rhoads General Hospital in Utica. Named after the historic river that flowed through the city, Mohawk College's first registration totaled 1,314 students. The last of ACUNY's campuses, Sampson College, with an initial enrollment of 2,825 students, utilized the sprawling 2,597-acre Sampson Naval Training Center on Lake Seneca, one of the state's picturesque Finger Lakes.

The ACUNY offered its students the first half of a normal four-year program in the liberal arts, business administration, and engineering. Upon completion of this curriculum approximately half of the students transferred to degree-granting institutions, a remarkable transfer rate considering the character and age of ACUNY and the possibility that most students enrolled primarily because no other school would take them. At its peak ACUNY had over eight thousand students and by June 1950 had registered over fifteen thousand, eighty-eight percent of them veterans. The $490-per-year tuition ACUNY collected during the four years of its existence produced an unplanned surplus in its operations budget. ACUNY provided a valuable service. It was well planned and efficiently operated, and won the distinction of being the only college established for a brief and limited period to serve the G.I. Bill veterans.[31]

Besides the great numbers of New York State veterans seeking a college education, a number of other forces pressured Dewey and the state to consider the possibility of creating a state university. Other forces for change were: 1) the precedent of a state university in every other state, 2) the ethnic and religious discrimination charges against private schools, 3) the situation whereby New York City's four municipal colleges produced forty percent of the state's teachers but received no state funds, and 4) the upstate location of every state teachers college. On 4 February 1946, at the height of the fear that the number of veterans seeking admission to college would soon far outstrip existing facilities, and a month prior to the conference of private college presidents, Dewey asked the state legislature to establish a Temporary Commission on the Need of a State University. The legislature complied, and following a lengthy study the commission submitted its final report to the governor on 16 February 1948. Six weeks later Dewey signed into law the bill that created the State University of New York, or SUNY, as it came to be called. The legislation placed under a central administration the state's scattered teachers colleges, the two-year agricultural and technical institutions, the Maritime Academy, and the contract colleges at Alfred, Cornell, and Syracuse Universities. This was a total of thirty-two constituent units, but the measure also authorized SUNY's board of trustees to plan for two medical centers and "such four-year liberal arts colleges, professional and graduate schools, research centers or other facilities, including an integrated university on a single campus," as they believed advisable.[32]

When the state created SUNY in the spring of 1948, however, most observers could see the end of the veteran bulge. Without the push of veteran enrollment, Dewey, his successor Averill Harriman, and the state legislature adopted a cautious attitude toward SUNY. Throughout the 1950s, once Champlain College closed, SUNY offered a liberal arts curriculum only at small, out-of-the-way Harpur College.[33] It stopped short of establishing an engineering or fine arts college, a law school, or a doctoral program in the arts or sciences. SUNY's potential became apparent only after Nelson Rockefeller won the governorship in 1958. Faced with huge enrollment estimates for the 1960s, when the children born during the World War II baby boom would reach college age, Rockefeller directed an expansion program that changed the teachers colleges into liberal arts institutions, created four major universities, and in general attempted to build a state college and university system that would rival that of any state in the country. The presence of veteran students in 1946–1950 clearly was the decisive catalyst for SUNY's administrative birth.[34]

Of all the agencies and organizations concerned with the G.I. Bill, the colleges themselves had the most intimate contact with the veteran. After a college accepted a G.I. Bill veteran as a student it returned to the V.A. the certified copy of his Certificate of Eligibility and Entitlement, and sent a certified statement showing the name and length of the general course of study he pursued, the date his training commenced, the status of his enrollment (full- or part-time), and an itemized statement of the cost of his tuition, fees, books, and supplies. The V.A. required the college to report any change in the educational status of the veteran. Many colleges operated, under contract, V.A. counseling centers, but all had offices to handle veteran affairs. With rare exception, however, colleges found that their major administrative activities and problems stemmed from the unprecedented enrollment and its subsequent demands for beds, classroom chairs, professors, and above all, dollars.

Colleges responded to higher enrollments by increasing their budgets and adding to their faculties. But the increases and additions rarely matched the increase in the number of students. Between 1940 and 1948 enrollment across the country climbed by seventy-five percent while the number of faculty members rose by only fifty-two percent. Both public and private schools, consequently, consistently enrolled more students per course than they had before the war. In the public schools the problem was the shortage of professors, not money, because during the 1940s the tax-supported institutions actually increased their expenditures per student (after adjustment for inflation). Between 1940 and 1950, on the other hand, the private schools decreased their spending per student. During the decade the public professional schools, for example, registered an eight percent increase in their spending per student, while the private professional schools recorded an eighteen percent decline. In each category (university, liberal arts college, professional school, and junior college) private institutions still outspent public, but the difference had become markedly less, in fact almost nonexistent in the university category. The private school decrease in spending per student far outweighed the public school increase, with the result that higher education as a whole spent four percent less per student in 1950 than it had in 1940.[35]

Each college, public or private, seemed to have a different experience with its veterans, depending upon the institution's nature and traditions. At the University of North Dakota, for example, veterans displayed little enthusiasm for the student activities of the prewar years, while the veterans at Rutgers University vigorously revived "most of the elements of campus life that had been familiar to the prewar generation."[36] The University of Illinois maintained that the state financed about half of the direct cost of educating its veteran student; small, private Denison University, on the other hand, found its veteran program financially profitable. In 1950, when the veteran enrollment dropped, Denison lowered its admission standards because an additional 100 students would pay a total of $50,000 in tuition but would add only $3,000 to the school's budget. While enrollment at most state universities declined during the early 1950s, it remained steady at the University of Maryland.[37]

Brown University took an administrative and academic step few other colleges attempted. Like so many institutions, Brown hated to reject veterans seeking admission, even the seemingly unqualified applicants. So in September 1946 Brown organized a Veterans College with a faculty drawn from the regular staff. All of the 486 veterans enrolled lacked the normally accepted entrance credentials. Many of them had taken commercial or vocational courses of study in high school, while others had barely earned their diplomas. The original plan called for these marginal students to spend two years in Veterans College, after which the good risks could transfer to the regular university. They attended afternoon or evening classes that only occasionally contained regular students. Meanwhile, they could not engage in extracurricular activities. The ages of the veterans ranged from twenty to thirty-eight, with an average of twenty-three. Most of them had applied to other schools but had failed to gain admission. Samuel T. Arnold, dean of the university, admitted that Brown established the Veterans College from a sense of duty and with considerable misgiving.

From the beginning the veterans astonished Brown officials. Upon entrance they took the same battery of tests as the regular students: the American Council on Education Psychological Examination, the Iowa English Test, and the Cooperative Mathematics Examination. Half of the veteran students scored as well as the upper three-quarters of the regular freshmen. At the end of the fall semester, 139 of the veterans had performed so well that Brown transferred them to regular status. This was three semesters earlier than planned. The experiment, in addition to contributing another compliment to veteran scholarship, illustrated how one college reacted in an unusual manner to a segment of veteran applicants.[38]

Negro colleges continued to suffer more than any other category of higher-learning institutions. With three exceptions, they were located in the seventeen southern states and the District of Columbia, which in 1940 contained seventy-nine percent of the nation's Negro citizens and which by law segregated all educational facilities. Less than five percent of these colleges enjoyed accreditation by the Association of American Universities. No school had an accredited engineering department or a graduate program at the doctoral level, and seven states had no graduate program at all. Half of the Negro colleges had fewer than 250 students. Southern Negro elementary and secondary schools, moreover, lacking adequate budgets, teachers, and support, generally sent to college students less prepared than the graduates of the separate and unequal white schools. The Negro colleges rested at the bottom of the collegiate academic hierarchy, the poorest colleges in the poorest educational region of the country.

Because of the G.I. Bill, the postwar enrollment at the Negro colleges, which in 1940 was 43,003 and ten years later reached 76,600, strained the collective physical plant to the breaking point. Limited facilities forced the colleges, during 1946 and 1947, to turn away an estimated 20,000 veterans. But since the G.I. Bill gave Negro veterans the financial means to attend college outside of the South, the percentage of veterans at the Negro colleges remained lower than the percentage of veterans at other institutions.[39] The Veterans' Educational Facilities Program, which distributed surplus war buildings and equipment to colleges, eased some of the pressure that record enrollments placed on classrooms and dormitories. The Federal Works Agency, recognizing the conditions of the Negro colleges, awarded the institutions a disproportionate amount of aid. Negro colleges had approximately 8.6 percent of the enrollment in colleges that participated in the program, but they received 14 percent of the total square feet of buildings. For each veteran, other colleges received an average of 17.4 square feet, while the Negro colleges received 33.4 square feet of floor space. The cost per square foot was $93 for white veterans and $156 for Negro veterans. Surplus war buildings boosted by twenty-five percent the physical plant of the Negro colleges and continued to serve succeeding college generations.[40]

Despite the extra buildings and slight enrollment variance, the Negro colleges' experience with the G.I. Bill veterans followed a pattern familiar to other colleges. There were too many students for facilities and there was no major structural change of programs or administrations. At the end of the veteran era the Negro colleges still held the same position in higher education that they had a decade earlier.

The basic unit in the G.I. Bill's operational or administrative hierarchy was, of course, the individual veteran. He received and spent approximately seventy percent of the five and one-half billion dollars the program cost; his choice of school shaped enrollment patterns and the associated problems; and his performance determined public acceptance and support of the entire G.I. Bill.

Individual veterans, like the administrative units, had their particular characteristics and problems. Two of the most distinguishable common characteristics of veteran students were their age and their marital status. Upon termination of the G.I. Bill the V.A. reported that the average veteran had been twenty-five years old when he entered college training, with fifty-six percent under twenty-five years and seventeen percent over thirty years. Between 1946 and 1949, however, the more prominent colleges recorded an average age for all veteran students that was lower than the age the V.A. found in its study. In June 1946, for example, the average age of veterans at the University of Illinois was 23.8 years; at the University of Pennsylvania the average in October 1946 was 24.4 years. And during the spring semester of 1947 a table of veteran ages at U.C.L.A. indicated that only 22.4 percent of all veterans were over twenty-five years old.[41]

Half of all the veterans who attended college on the G.I. Bill were married. Their older age undoubtedly accounted for many marriages, but the G.I. Bill made student marriages financially compatible with college attendance. Of the married veterans, half had one or more children.[42] The married veterans, whether because of added

Table 3

CHARACTERISTICS OF WORLD WAR II G.I. BILL ENROLLMENT
IN VARIOUS TRAINING PROGRAMS

| Program | Number | % Total | Average age on entering | % of Trainees w/Dependents | | |
				none	one	more than one
On the farm	700,000	9	29	14	26	60
Below college	3,500,000	44	28	42	23	35
On the job	1,400,000	18	26	25	42	33
College	2,200,000	29	25	50	24	26
All programs	15,400,000	1000	27	38	27	35

Source: Information Bulletin 7-106, 6 June 1956, pp. 2, 16, 18, Vocational
Rehabilitation and Education Division, V.A.

responsibility or greater maturity, earned higher grades than their
bachelor peers and thereby proved that marital status need not handicap
a student.

Veterans faced two major nonacademic problems, housing and
finances. As early as January 1946 the American Council on Education
reported that 87 of the 100 leading colleges had inadequate student
housing. The lack of housing tested the resourcefulness of college
officials and students, often with imaginative and colorful results. The
single veteran, because of his access to housing in surplus military
quarters and in other federal housing projects, actually had an easier
time finding a bed than did his nonveteran classmate. Colleges usually
gave veterans priority in campus housing. Conditions were crowded
and often unusual. At the University of Illinois three hundred veterans
paid $8.50 a month to sleep in bunk beds in the Old Gymnasium
Annex. Veterans at Indiana University slept on cots in locker rooms,
gymnasiums, and dormitory halls. Meanwhile, Alabama Polytechnic
Institute obtained ninety-three tugboats from the United States Maritime
Commission and veterans bunked by twos in each of their cabins.
With New York State underwriting the cost, Rensselaer Polytechnic
Institute moored four surplus LST's (Landing Ship Tanks) in the Hudson
River where 600 veterans established floating dormitories.[43]

Improvisation also helped the married veterans, but because of
their special housing needs they confronted a more serious housing
situation than their single counterparts. Thanks to the various federal
agencies and sympathetic college officials, married veterans moved
into military and defense facilities located within commuting distance
and into the wide array of prefabricated buildings and trailers brought
to the campuses. Some of Harvard's married veterans lived in apartments

at Fort Devens but others lived on the top six floors of Boston's Brunswick Hotel, which the University obtained for that purpose. At all-male Dartmouth, Williams, Hamilton, and Princeton the married veterans moved into apartments converted from dormitories. At Columbia University fourteen veteran families lived in a mansion built by Alexander Hamilton's son. Diversity abounded. Some veterans lived with their parents while others built houses for themselves. Two brothers at Lehigh University and their families shared an eight room farm house one had purchased. In Berkeley, California, on the other hand, three families crammed into a five room bungalow.[44]

The married veterans, especially those living in the trailer towns, Quonset villages, and other "vetsvilles," quickly developed a subculture within the college environment. Wives' organizations, nursery schools, baby-sitting exchanges, self-government units, and even food cooperatives sprang up on campuses across the nation. Similar ages, experiences, interests, housing, and incomes generated a strong sense of community. Although the trailers lacked plumbing, the streets often were muddy, and almost all the apartments were small and poorly heated, the overwhelming majority of veterans and their wives felt that the advantages of their circumstances far outweighed the disadvantages. Many undoubtedly agreed with the wife who concluded that the time her husband spent as a college student constituted "three of the happiest years we had known." Three-fourths of the 544 married veterans polled at Michigan State College (now Michigan State University) replied affirmatively to the question, "Knowing what you now know, would you marry before finishing college if you were unmarried?" At the State University of Iowa every veteran, married and unmarried, felt he had done "the right thing in going to college."[45]

Like almost all students, veterans had financial problems, but for several reasons they had a special psychological need to be self-supporting. They were older, had been financially independent while in service, and half of them were married. Although the veteran program went a long way toward fulfilling the psychological and dollar needs of veterans, its checks met the total expenses of only a few of them. Until 1 April 1948 monthly subsistence checks were $65 for single and $90 for married veterans. After that date the amounts increased to $75 and $105, with a new rate of $120 for the veteran with two or more dependents. But in June 1947 the Social Research Laboratory at City College of New York reported after a six-month study that the average single veteran spent $84.95 monthly and the average married veteran spent $181.92 to live "with a minimum of comfort." The same semester, at Rensselaer Polytechnic Institute in Troy, New York, single veterans spent $103.32 a month and married veterans $150.70 a month. And across the country at Stanford University the financial story read similarly: $120 for single and $180 for married veterans.[46]

With a pronounced difference between G.I. Bill income and living expenses, veterans resorted to loans, savings, family gifts, and work to balance their budgets. In Iowa City, veteran students constituted eighty percent of the community's janitorial force. At CCNY forty-three percent of the married and thirty-three percent of the single veterans worked part-time. Of the married veterans at Stanford, nearly two-thirds had wives who worked, while almost half of the married veterans at Michigan State had working wives. Veterans met their financial needs in the same manner as did other college students, with two exceptions: they relied less on parental support and many had wives who worked.[47]

Individual veterans, of course, were not administrators. They were the beneficiaries of the administrative process that included countless college officials, V.A. clerks and officers, federal agencies, and congressional committees. No one person or office held an inordinate amount of power, and therefore, there was no key or prominent person associated with the program. The colleges, because they provided the services upon which the entire program rested, were the key to understanding the operation of the G.I. Bill.

5. The University of Wisconsin: A Case Study

U.W. Will Admit All Students It Can House

Headlines in *The Daily Cardinal*, May 1946.

For the past four years we have gone "all out" to be of service to the ex-G.I.s who came to us in such overwhelming numbers following the close of World War II. . . . Nor has the transaction been all one-sided. Our 30,000 student veterans have been a stabilizing influence on Wisconsin student life. Their maturity has enabled them to raise scholarship levels. Their greater sense of responsibility has improved student-faculty relationships.

E. B. Fred, Report of the President, November 1950.

FROM 1946 to 1950 students who were veterans of World War II dominated the University of Wisconsin. During these years the majority of male students were veterans, and for the first three years of this period veterans constituted the majority of all students. Older and more experienced than any previous college generation, veterans earned higher grades than nonveteran students, shattered enrollment records, intensified traditional administrative problems, and created a colorful social and intellectual chapter in the university's history.

Early in World War II the faculty formally expressed its awareness that veterans would enroll at the university after their military service ended, and that because of their experience veterans deserved special treatment. At their meeting of 9 February 1942, the faculty approved a motion which granted ten elective college credits to former enlisted men and fifteen credits to former officers who had served in the military for more than three months.[1] Two years later, when it was evident that Congress would provide financial assistance to veterans who wished to return to school, the faculty Steering Committee on Post-war University Problems recommended that the university create a separate committee to deal with special educational problems of veterans. In making its recommendation, the steering committee suggested two guidelines for the university to follow in its treatment of veterans: 1) "The general policy of the University should be to absorb the war veterans into the general student body as far as possible and to organize separate courses and provide special services only as the desirability for these is clearly evident," and 2) the university "should permit a maximum of flexibility in such matters as entrance requirements, attainment examinations and substitution of courses or the earning of credit by examination, but without any lowering of the standards of quality."[2] The faculty, administration, and regents accepted the committee's guidelines, which established the basis for university treatment of veterans and which proved wise and successful. The Committee on Veteran Education appointed by President Clarence A. Dystra served as a coordinating agency to carry out the policy recommendations of the faculty steering committee in matters of admission, organization of special courses and services, academic placement, counseling, and instruction of veterans.

The special consideration and assistance veterans received was divided into two categories: education and service. In March 1944 the faculty approved a long list of preferential educational considerations. For example, if a veteran had fewer than the sixteen high school units required for admission, he could substitute four of the fifteen special war credits for each unit he lacked, and if this were still insufficient, he could apply on a war-veteran basis and be admitted upon providing satisfactory evidence, oral or perhaps a written qualifying examination, that he was capable of doing college work. Veterans could apply toward a degree certain college-level work completed in service schools and in military training programs. Veterans were exempt from the military science and physical education courses which were compulsory for other students. The faculty stipulated that a veteran's record of deficiency at any university or college during the term preceding induction into the armed forces would not be the cause of ineligibility for intercollegiate athletics or other extracurricular activities. As an emergency measure to accelerate training, the faculty lowered the requirement for entrance into the Medical School from three to two years of premedical work. Beginning with the fall semester of 1945, the university created a special eight-week session to run concurrently with the last half of each semester to enable veterans, and other qualified students, to start or resume their studies at more than the traditional beginning dates. The university offered refresher courses in such fields as mathematics, agriculture, commerce, and English. To help veterans reduce the time needed to complete their degrees, the university established a full semester summer school. The Engineering College operated on a trimester schedule with semesters starting in March, July, and November. The Law and Medical Schools offered their own refresher courses for students whose education had been interrupted or for those graduates who experienced a gap between completion of their education and their entry into practice. The ultimate in special consideration for the veteran existed in the preference given to his admission over that of any other student.[3]

In addition to special academic treatment, the university also provided veterans with special nonacademic services. Initially, the Office of Personnel Council cared for veteran records, counseled veterans, and maintained liaison with state agencies concerned with veterans. As the number of veterans returning to campus increased, the university established in the autumn of 1945 the Office of Veteran Affairs (OVA) and the Veterans Business Office (VBO). The OVA counseled university veterans as to their rights and privileges under state and federal law and assisted them in application to, changes in, and problems of their educational program. This office, which in 1946 employed the time of one and one-half men, also conducted liaison duties with the V.A. (regional office, local office, hospital, guidance center), the Governor's Educational Advisement Committee, and the Wisconsin Department of Veteran Affairs (WDVA). To serve better as a referral agency and an information headquarters, the OVA published a free monthly newspaper, *Veterans' News Digest*, "to disseminate news of interest to the veteran attending the University." The VBO certified veteran enrollment, withdrawals, courses of study, book and other costs, and worked closely with the university business office. The university further assisted the veteran by operating on campus, under a V.A. contract, a counseling unit which provided testing and counseling for any veteran (not limited to university students) assigned by the V.A. Professional help at the unit was mandatory for veterans who made excessive program changes or performed unsatisfactorily, but was available to all veterans upon request.[4]

At all times the university cooperated with governmental and private organizations designed to aid veterans. The WDVA based its decisions for loans and supplementary grants to needy veterans solely upon the recommendations of the OVA. Since the first monthly subsistence checks arrived weeks after classes started (the majority of veterans enrolled for the first time often waited until November), the university permitted veterans to postpone payment for books, supplies, tuition, and fees, provided they had V.A. certificates of eligibility for benefits under the G.I. Bill. If a veteran had applied for, but had not yet received, this certificate, the WDVA would underwrite the credit for a Wisconsin resident, and the Red Cross for a nonresident, until it arrived, at which time the university assumed the obligation.[5]

The university created little new administrative machinery to handle the veterans. Whenever possible it utilized existing personnel and agencies and avoided unnecessary academic and administrative distinction between veterans and nonveterans. The veteran applied to the same admission office as the nonveteran, secured his living accommodations from the same housing bureau, and paid his fees through an adjunct of the regular business office. At all times, the university expected the faculty, through its academic advisory program, to be the major influence on all students. In the crucial areas of advising and teaching, faculty made no distinction between veterans and non-veterans. To be sure, the veteran enjoyed priorities of administrative and academic services which helped him to enroll in the university, but the priority stopped at the classroom door. By its cooperation with nonuniversity organizations concerned with veterans; by its flexible requirements and programs, generous educational benefits, and special courses; and by its administrative services, the university carried out the original recommendations of the faculty Steering Committee on

Post-war University Problems to absorb the veterans into the student body and to maintain educational flexibility.

Establishing educational guidelines and administrative services, however time consuming, proved easy compared with estimating how many veterans would enroll at the university and predicting how they would adjust to academic life. In his letter, "Dear Badger in Service," dated 5 May 1945, President E. B. Fred candidly wrote that "we do not know how many students will enroll after the war, but estimates have ranged as high as 18,000." The following January, with about 9,000 students on campus, Registrar J. Kenneth Little believed that the university could absorb only 12,500 of the 15,000 candidates he expected to apply for September 1946. But in September the enrollment climbed to 18,598, with over 10,000 out-of-state applicants turned away, three-quarters of them veterans. This record-breaking figure created visions of even more students. In November 1946 the *Daily Cardinal* predicted "over 24,000" students in September 1947 while Registrar Little concluded that enrollment would reach only 23,000 and President Fred estimated but 20,000. Rather than additional thousands of students in September 1947, the university recorded about one hundred more than the previous year. The next month President Fred cautiously told the faculty that "the huge wave of veterans going to college has probably reached its peak." He was right. Enrollment remained stable for two years and then slid to its postwar low in 1953–1954.[6]

The analysis of enrollment statistics, in addition to demonstrating the gap between expectation and realization, reveals the abnormality of veteran enrollment. Between the spring of 1944 and the autumn of 1946 the influx of veterans tripled the number of students on campus, surpassing the record numbers of 1938 by sixty-three percent (see Table 4). In September 1946 freshmen, the majority of whom were veterans, constituted 33.2 percent of the total university enrollment, while the senior class amounted to only 13.4 percent. Three years later the senior class accounted for 24.8 percent of university enrollment and the freshmen class only 17 percent. Law, Medicine, and Graduate School enrollments reflected a similar pattern.[7] Not until September 1960 did total enrollment equal and pass what it had been thirteen years earlier. To accommodate the increased numbers of Wisconsin veterans, the university restricted out-of-state undergraduate enrollment. From a high of thirty-four percent nonresident undergraduates in 1945, the percentage dropped to ten in 1947, but by 1959 had climbed to twenty-three. Enrollment in the Graduate School soon

Table 4

UNIVERSITY OF WISCONSIN ENROLLMENT FOR SELECTED YEARS, 1938-1954

Year (First semester)	Total Enrollment	Male Enrollment	Veteran Enrollment
1938–1939	11,416	8,394	–
1943–1944	5,904	1,951	Approx. 50
1944–1945	6,615	2,011	260
1945–1946	9,028	5,315	1,347
1946–1947	18,598	13,458	11,076
1947–1948	18,693	13,905	10,792
1948–1949	18,623	14,095	10,134
1949–1950	17,690	13,345	7,938
1950–1951	15,766	11,540	5,455
1951–1952	14,020	9,977	3,535
1952–1953	13,571	9,518	2,215*
1953–1954	13,346	9,192	1,422†
1954–1955	13,954	9,741	1,067‡

Source: File 19/11/3/00–1, University of Wisconsin Archives.
*Plus 234 Korean veterans and 157 World War II-Korean veterans.
†Plus 873 Korean veterans and 204 World War II-Korean veterans.
‡Plus 1,820 Korean veterans and 207 World War II-Korean veterans.

reflected both the increased numbers of Wisconsin natives who earned undergraduate degrees and the decline in the numbers of nonresident students who did. In 1948, 64.4 percent of graduate students were nonresidents, but as more Wisconsin veterans completed degrees and entered Graduate School, the percentage fell to 60.1 in 1951, fluctuated, and then fell further to 57.2 in 1958. In 1938 the university awarded 1,523 bachelor's degrees; in 1949 it awarded 3,404.[8]

On the subject of veteran adjustment to civilian and academic life, university officials generally remained publicly silent; those who did comment expressed apprehension. In July 1944, for example, W. W. Blaesser, assistant dean of men, told a Student Board meeting that the university needed to do a better job of veteran rehabilitation, and requested the help of student organizations. The majority of the veterans already on campus, he maintained, found adjustment to college difficult; they were restless, uneasy, and uncertain to study habits. "Most of the veterans," he insisted, "are used to being told what to do and find it difficult adjusting to a situation where they have to go out on their own. They're shy." Blaesser also warned of the strong possibility of increased racial problems due to the experiences of veterans. Early in 1945 the Student Board and its War Council discussed the problem of "social orientation" of discharged service men. Harry Rosenbaum, War Council chairman, suggested a plan that would have members of Interfraternity Council meet veterans as they stepped off their trains and then serve as big-brother guides.[9]

The expected problems, however, never materialized. Lawrence O'Neill, Jr., an undergraduate major in journalism and a veteran of twenty-seven bombing raids over Europe, published his view of university veterans and confirmed for a larger audience the opinion expressed so frequently on campus. In *The Wisconsin Alumnus*, O'Neill remarked that "contrary to all advance notices, the veteran has had no problem in adjusting himself to college life. . . . I can't think of a single acquaintance who has ever mentioned such a problem." [10]

In addition to observation, veteran adjustment also could be measured by academic achievement. During the autumn semester of 1945–1946, the first time the number of veterans became statistically important, undergraduate veteran men earned higher grade point averages than nonveterans in every school and every class, with the exception of the senior class, in which averages for the two groups differed 2.017 to 2.015. The same favorable comparison continued throughout the peak veteran years, with married veterans consistently at the top of the honor roll. Typical was the spring semester of 1946–1947 when 8,766 male undergraduate veterans earned a 1.673 grade point average compared to a 1.582 average achieved by their 1,550 nonveteran classmates. Married veterans, living in university housing projects, with children compiled a 1.788 average while those married without children earned a 1.826.[11] One study of 114 veterans, whose military service interrupted their college education, tabulated that ninety-nine improved their academic performance, six indicated no change, and nine registered a decline of grade point average.[12] The impressive academic performance of veterans caused LeRoy Luberg, assistant to President Fred, to declare that the "scholastic competition" at the university in 1947 was "much keener" than before the war. And if drop-out rate is taken as another indication of veteran adjustment, servicemen made the transition to college more easily than did the traditional high school graduate, since a comparison of the drop-out rate of the two groups consistently favored the veteran.[13]

The majority of veterans obviously arrived on campus with a serious attitude toward their studies, but contrary to expectations, this did not mean they flocked to "practical" programs and avoided the liberal arts. A comparison of veteran and nonveteran members of the class of 1949 indicated just the opposite (see Table 5), and

Table 5

PERCENTAGE OF UNIVERSITY OF WISCONSIN
CLASS OF 1949
IN SPECIFIC COLLEGES

College	Veterans (2,652)	Non veterans (825)
Liberal Arts	38.1%	25.5%
Education	10.3%	6.1%
Commerce	13.9%	44.0%
Engineering	27.6%	16.0%
Agriculture	10.1%	8.4%

Source: File 19/11/3/00–1, University of Wisconsin Archives.

statistics for veteran enrollment in the Graduate School reflected the same pattern.[14]

The veterans had no problem with adjustment; in fact, their maturity and adaptiveness drew praise. In the autumn of 1950 President Fred summarized the widely shared consensus that "veterans have been a stabilizing influence on Wisconsin student life. Their maturity has enabled them to raise scholarship levels. Their greater sense of responsibility has improved student-faculty relationships." [15]

The traditional problems of administering the university—finances, faculty, and physical plant—reached gargantuan dimensions during the veteran years. During the immediate postwar years the relationship between the university's enrollment, budget, and state appropriations (see Table 6) vividly illustrated the financial situation of the university. Veterans doubled enrollment between September 1945 and September 1946, for example, but the state reduced by seven percent its contribution to the university's budget. And when the legislature did become more generous with its appropriations, inflation absorbed some of the benefit.

To obtain additional income and to adjust for inflation, the university raised its semester fees from $48 in 1945 to $60 in 1947, and then to $75 in 1949. Nonresident tuition per semester increased from $148 to $225 during the same period.

The biggest boost to the university's budget (except for increased state appropriations) during these years came from the G.I. Bill tuition provision which stipulated that the government program would pay to universities and colleges the cost of instruction for each veteran, up to $500 a year. Since the nonresident tuition more nearly reflected the cost of education than did the resident fee, the university, with full cooperation and approval of the Veterans' Administration, charged

Table 6

UNIVERSITY OF WISCONSIN ENROLLMENT, BUDGET, AND LEGISLATIVE
APPROPRIATIONS, 1939-1954

Year	Enrollment	Budget	Appropriations
1939-1940	11,286	9,319,763	3,740,165
1940-1941	11,376	9,508,578	3,583,140
1941-1942	10,571	10,087,406	3,965,748
1942-1943	9,026	10,445,091	3,976,215
1943-1944	5,904	11,905,495	4,379,843
1944-1945	6,615	11,505,087	4,281,464
1945-1946	9,028	13,270,712	6,026,556
1946-1947	18,598	18,003,863	5,610,585
1947-1948	18,693	25,934,378	7,903,757
1948-1949	18,623	26,303,109	10,001,329
1949-1950	17,690	27,976,301	9,612,484
1950-1951	15,766	28,943,143	11,775,947
1951-1952	14,020	31,469,853	12,891,237
1952-1953	13,571	32,999,838	15,242,864
1953-1954	13,346	34,510,798	11,291,661
1954-1955	13,954	36,321,417	14,516,422

Source: File 19/11/3/00-1, University of Wisconsin Archives.

nonresident tuition to Wisconsin citizens who served in World War
II.[16] The additional income from tuition gained in this manner amounted
to $939,800 for the fall semester of 1946 alone, and for the veteran
years totaled about $10,000,000.

The university solved its teacher problem by increasing the size
of classes and by utilizing persons with incompleted training, primarily
graduate students. Classes doubled and tripled their prewar size and
public address systems in class became common. The number of faculty
at all ranks also set new records, but the most significant increase
came at the lowest positions (see Table 7).

The number of graduate assistants and instructors more than
doubled, increases of 111 percent and 108 percent. Meanwhile, the
number of assistant professors increased by 54 percent, associate
professors and professors by 41 percent during the same eight-year
period. In 1939-1940 professors constituted 13.9 percent and graduate
assistants 37.4 percent of the total faculty; in 1947-1948 the percentages
were 10.6 and 42.9 percent. The patterns established during the veteran
era—increased class size, greater use of graduate assistants as faculty,
and the corresponding decrease in percentage of professorial-level
faculty—remained after the veterans graduated. By 1962-1963 the

Table 7

UNIVERSITY OF WISCONSIN FACULTY

Rank	1939–1940	1947–1948
Professors	247	347
Associate professors	155	218
Assistant professors	216	332
Instructors	418	870
Graduate assistants	665	1,402

Source: Bulletin of the University of Wisconsin, November 1940, p. 404; ibid., September 1949, p. 512.

Not listed are lecturers (1939–1940, 46; 1947–1948, 62); associates (1939–1940, 17; 1947–1948, 27); deans (1939–1940, 10; 1947–1948, 9); registrar (1 each year); and the president.

percentage of professorial faculty had fallen further from the figures of 1939–1940.

The most serious problem caused by the postwar enrollment was the demand on the physical plant. For three years it was the availability of beds, on campus and in the greater Madison area, and of classroom space that limited enrollment, not the university budget, not the educational guidelines, and certainly not the scarcity of qualified applicants. With a limited physical plant and a determination to maintain prewar admission requirements for Wisconsin residents, the university took the only possible action: it banned out-of-state students. Initially, the university restricted the number of out-of-state women, but in January 1946, the faculty voted to ban all nonresident, nonveteran students, stated that the policy was temporary, and blamed the housing shortage. The only new out-of-state students permitted were scholarship holders, persons married to admitted students, and a few veterans with "unusual high aptitude" for college work. During the summer of 1948 the university relaxed its nonresident ban, but not until 1951 did the Medical School again open its doors to nonresidents. Enrollment curtailment helped, but relative to the total enrollment problem, it was only a beginning.[17]

To provide needed classroom space, the university lengthened its operating schedule, utilized temporary buildings, and campaigned for a construction program to provide adequate permanent buildings. In addition to operating the campus on a year-round basis, with a full semester during the summer session, the university scheduled classes from 7:45 A.M. to 9:30 P.M.

The use of temporary structures proved the most valuable mitigator for the pressures exerted on the physical plant. Between the summer of 1946 and Thanksgiving 1947, construction crews erected thirty-nine assorted prefabricated buildings on vacant areas around the campus. Among the first were seven Quonset huts placed adjacent to the State Historical Society, six of which divided into two classrooms each. The seventh Quonset housed the library's reserve book reading room, replacing its smaller predecessor in the Bascom Hall basement. The School of Commerce moved into two large barracks located immediately behind Bascom Hall. A third barracks in the Bascom Hall area provided general classrooms. Three barracks on the front lawn of Barnard dormitory contained classrooms and labs. In late October 1947 two buildings on the corner of Breeze Terrace and University Avenue opened as a 400-seat cafeteria to relieve lines over 200 yards long at the union cafeteria. The prefabs were unsightly and often poorly ventilated and heated, but they were cheap, could be pressed into quick service, and made available 145,662 square feet of floor space.[18]

The crowded physical plant reflected both record enrollment and the limitations of prewar facilities. After the construction of Sterling Hall in 1916, for example, the College of Letters and Science gained almost no permanent space until after the veteran era. In his message at the opening session of the 1945 state legislature on 3 January, Governor Walter S. Goodland pointed out that except for the Medical School buildings and the mechanical engineering buildings, there had been no major addition to the academic plant of the university for nearly thirty years. He instructed the legislature to meet the problem "squarely and adequately" and to do so in "a far sighted and statesman like way." [19] The legislature responded with an appropriation of eight million dollars for construction and equipment of new buildings. Additional funds, however, came slowly. In the fall of 1947 the university published the results of a study which showed that classroom space per student during the previous thirty years had decreased from 5,300 to 2,600 cubic feet. "The Regents and faculty agreed, after a careful study of the campus," the booklet read, "that at least 49 building projects are necessary to give the university the space it needs for its program of teaching and research." [20] Two months later President Fred reported to the legislature that "at present prices, the necessary additions to the University plant would cost a minimum of $60,000,000," and reminded its members that the previous spring they had appropriated only two million dollars after the Regents had requested nine million for immediate building needs and five million annually thereafter. On 2 May 1949, the faculty unanimously approved a resolution that warned the legislature "the University for too long has suffered from lack of adequate space and modern facilities. Unbelievably crowded and hazardous conditions must be rectified progressively and promptly if quality in teaching, scholarship, and research is to be maintained." A new library, the resolution insisted, "cannot longer be deferred." The *Daily Cardinal* seconded the desperate need for a new library, commented that 1,250,000 books jammed a building designed for 675,000 volumes, and asked for more than 700 library seats for 17,000 students.[21]

Finally, in 1949 and 1950 the legislature appropriated sufficient funds to embark the university on a building program that President Fred called the greatest "in the 101-year history of the institution." In November 1950 Fred summarized that since 1945 seventeen permanent buildings at a cost of $21,409,000 and seven projects "closely associated with the University but not. . . strictly University buildings" at a cost of $12,808,000, "either have been completed, are in the process of construction, or are on the drawing boards." [22] Of the $34,217,000 construction budget, $15,460,000 represented state appropriations. Among the major buildings financed by the state were the Memorial Library (ground finally broken July 1950), Babcock Hall (dairy and food technology center), general engineering building, an addition to the hospital, and the Bacteriology Building. In 1947 the Wisconsin Alumni Research Foundation (WARF) gave the university a 150-unit faculty housing project, the income from which endowed professorships. Two years later WARF financed the university's Enzyme Institute and later contributed to a new chemical engineering building. The University of Wisconsin Foundation made the university a gift of the $2,250,000 Wisconsin Center building.[23] Despite this construction and the even greater building program of the 1960s, prefab units, originally designed for ten years of service, still are found on campus, bleak, functional reminders of an earlier period.

Of all the problems an inadequate physical plant created, none equaled the magnitude of the housing shortage. The headlines of the *Daily Cardinal* on 3 May 1946 revealed the seriousness: "UW Will Admit All Students It Can House." The want ads of the Madison newspapers further documented the shortage, and the tents set up on the corner of Park Street and University Avenue to provide veterans a place to sleep while searching for a room dramatized the situation.

To alleviate the housing shortage, the university leased and purchased a wide range of temporary facilities, including trailers, overnight cabins, sites for students to park their own trailers, Quonset huts, part of an air base, and part of an ordnance plant.

The first temporary housing provided by the university was a trailer park for veterans placed on the lawns and practice fields of Camp Randall, the parklike area containing the football stadium, field house, and Civil War monuments. Named Randall Park and opened in September 1945, the furnished one-room units required residents to carry water from one of four utilities buildings, which also provided communal bathrooms, washing machines, and ironing boards. For their trailers and utilities, veterans paid $25.00 a month, $32.50 if they occupied the larger of the two sizes available. Although the university leased the trailers from the Federal Public Housing Authority for a dollar a year and operated the park on a nonprofit basis, the cost of moving, renovating, providing sewers, roads, water, electricity, and maintenance forced the university to set the rents at the above figures. Paramount News and Acme News photographed life in the park for its movie newsreels and shipped the film across the country and around the world. *Life* and *Look* magazines also published pictures and comments about Randall Park. Much of the national interest may be explained by the newness of the project; Randall Park was one of the first, if not the first, "vetsville" on a college campus. As long as the university maintained temporary housing for married veterans, the trailers at convenient Randall Park topped the list of preferred assignments.[24]

Randall Park was only the first step in providing housing for married veterans. In January and February 1946, veterans moved into 113 additional trailers placed adjacent to Randall Park. Beginning the summer of 1946, the university spent $85,000 to construct a trailer park on the east end of the University Hill Farm, two miles west of campus, providing sites for 125 veteran-owned trailers. In September 1946 the university paid $35,000 for the Sullivan overnight cabins on University Avenue, and immediately added twenty-four trailer sites and four Quonset huts to the original sixteen, one-room cabins.[25]

The university maintained its two largest housing projects miles from campus. During the autumn of 1945, with housing scarce and becoming more so, the university petitioned the federal government to use as veteran housing portions of Truax Field, a communications training center six miles from campus, and portions of the Badger Ordnance Works, a munitions complex thirty-five miles away in Sauk County.

Following quick government approval, almost 500 veterans moved in the partially ready Truax facilities in January 1946, and by September the area housed almost 1,200 veterans in forty-six buildings or building wings, each named after a university alumnus killed during the war.

Opened as part of the Division of Residence Halls, the self-contained community included a post office, cafeteria, gymnasium, library, theater, and service club. The Truax project, with room rents ranging from $13 to $19.50, remained open until June 1950 but always lacked kitchen facilities needed to accommodate couples with children.[26]

To solve the housing shortage for married veterans with children, the university opened Badger Village in January 1946 and operated the project until April 1952.[27] The Federal Public Housing Authority, to whom the university relinquished control, permitted students to live at the village until June 1953. Named after the ordnance works constructed in 1942–1943, Badger Village had a capacity of 699 families and included a post office (Badger, Wisconsin), fire company, drug store, chapel, grocery store, community building, barber shop, and elementary school (kindergarten through eighth grade). Rental costs varied from $17.50 to $29.50. Operating at capacity for several years, usually with a waiting list, the village housed 408 veteran families even as late as 1950.[28]

Veterans accepted the university's make-shift housing with rare complaint. All the housing projects formed local governments to handle community affairs. They also organized and supported a wide variety of social and cultural activities. The trailer areas established cooperative food stores. And the university provided various services to all projects, especially bus transportation for Truax and Badger Village residents.

World War II veterans blended into and soon dominated extracurricular activities on campus with as much ease and achievement as they demonstrated in the classroom. As a rule, veterans filled student offices across campus in greater proportion than their number.

They also joined fraternities, but their membership, while a financial asset, contributed to the change in tradition of the Greek-lettered organizations that had begun during the depression of the 1930s. Veterans joined fraternities for many reasons, some new to the Greek system. With housing at a premium, some joined mainly to have a bed, dresser, and desk near campus. Others, especially married veterans, affiliated chiefly to satisfy recreational needs. To accommodate demand, some fraternities markedly increased their memberships. Theta Delta Chi, for example, listed nineteen members in 1940 and eighty in 1948. The increased membership helped to undermine the brotherhood theme of fraternities. There was a greater age and interest range than before. Chapters felt compelled to sponsor a wider social program to please the brothers not living in the house because of limited accommodations or marital status. Resident members often

felt they ran a social center, not a fraternal organization. More important
was the attitude of the veterans. Germany's slaughter of millions of
Jews made the ethnic and religious discrimination clauses of fraternity
constitutions repugnant to many veterans. A favorite topic of debate
on the nation's campuses during the postwar years was whether
fraternities and sororities should be abolished. And at the time fraternities experienced attack, veterans constituted a strong majority of
membership, and they never felt the respect and loyalty for the
organization as did nineteen- or twenty-year-olds. Inflation, world
affairs, and national politics proved more compelling considerations.
A generation of students, probably the most respected in the nation's
history, therefore, viewed fraternities from a different perspective than
traditional high school graduates did, and the veteran influence lin-
gered.[29]

The handful of veterans on campus during the autumn of 1944
formed the University of Wisconsin Veterans of World War II, an
organization whose aim was "to maintain good fellowship and understanding among all mankind, and to foster those rights for which
the people of our nation and of Allied countries are now engaged
in preserving in this war." According to Lee Alfgren, its first president,
the group was "the most progressive" veterans' association in the
country, one whose motto was "not what we can get, but what we
can give."[30] President Fred, the administration, and the faculty gave
unreserved support, including a Quonset hut east of the Student Union.

Despite its initial promise and the well-wishes of the university
community, the organization fell apart at the peak of veteran enrollment.
Students at Wisconsin traditionally have concerned themselves with
national and international affairs, and the veterans intensified this
concern. But as the numbers of veterans on campus increased, the
leadership of the organization seemed less and less aware of this tradition.
Before it was a year old, the group voted to avoid any issues which
might involve the organization in political controversy. The original
dedication to "all mankind" became instead a "main purpose . . .
to make the veterans independent on campus and to welcome and
encourage them to join in all the campus activities."[31] Since the Office
of Veterans Affairs provided veterans with information and the various
campus activities propagandized themselves, and since the veterans
needed little help with adjustment, the services offered by the group
essentially were weak duplications. Finally, in February 1947 Shirley
Kast, a news editor of the student paper, published a two-part article
about the group in which she attacked it as "the poorest excuse for

a veterans' organization in the nation," insisted that it was not representing Wisconsin veterans, and concluded that the club was poorly run.[32] During the controversy that followed, Leonard Kosinski, president, boasted that "the organization is conservative. Groups that delve into issues that seem to go beyond the campus destroy themselves. This group is stable."[33] Two and a half months later, the seven members present unanimously voted to dissolve the organization. Kosinski's conservative, stable organization which refused to concern itself with national affairs had attracted few veterans.

In October 1946 veterans on campus organized the David Schreiner Post, No. 520 of the American Legion, but the post failed to sponsor a program that attracted many veterans. The most newsworthy event associated with the post was its commander's public denunciation, at a campus Young Republicans meeting, of the proposal to increase veteran subsistence payment because he did not want to support persons who "were just too lazy to work." [34]

During the first week of August 1946 another group of university veterans formed a chapter of the nationwide American Veterans Committee and quickly won support of a meaningful number of veterans. Many members belonged to the Madison AVC chapter and logically moved onto campus to fill the void created when the University of Wisconsin Veterans of World War II organization showed signs of ineptness. In 1946 the AVC, though only two years old, counted close to 100,000 members and 700 chapters across the country, and dedicated its efforts to peace, employment, and freedom. The success of the university chapter rested upon its program of discussing national and world problems, its concern for veteran well-being on campus, and its leadership.

At its first meeting after organization, the executive board of the university AVC authorized its chairman, Russell Wright, to make a statement of policies. "First of all," Wright subsequently announced for the organization, "AVC believes that veterans can prosper only if the American people as a whole are prosperous." The group, therefore, supported price control, government action to maintain full employment, and "adequate low-cost housing." Wright added that veterans would enjoy "their freedom" only if the civil liberties of all Americans were maintained. "The only realistic solution of international problems," the AVC chairman reported, was "United Nations cooperation for durable peace eventually growing into world government." [35]

The commitment to consider fundamental problems, which characterized the AVC's first public statement, inaugurated the policy that continued throughout the chapter's existence on campus. From 1946 to 1950 the AVC passed resolutions and submitted petitions which supported the Acheson-Lilienthal report to place all atomic energy under international control, suggested the United Nations administer the Marshall Plan, and opposed universal military training. The AVC forum, occasionally broadcast over station WHA, discussed such topics as race discrimination, American foreign policy, price controls, and the Taft-Hartley Labor Act. On campus, the AVC demanded the university raise its pay scale for part-time student employment, opposed compulsory R.O.T.C., and supported increased faculty salaries. When the Three Bells Tavern refused to serve a Negro law student during the summer of 1947, the AVC organized a boycott and asked Madisonians to "practice a little real Americanism." [36] Although AVC refused to accept for membership communists and fascists, and endorsed the "private enterprise system," it denounced the "proposal to bar the local chapter of the American Youth for Democracy from the campus regardless of the political complexion of its membership," and attacked State Senator Bernard Gettelman's bill "to bar Communist students, faculty members, or regents" from association with the university.[37]

The AVC and its speakers, forums, and positions received wide support. Typical of the leadership the organization attracted were presidents John Higham, later professor of history at the University of Michigan, John A. Gronowski, later postmaster general of the United States and ambassador to Poland, and Ivan Nestigen, later mayor of Madison and United States undersecretary of health, education, and welfare. Veterans had no wish to isolate themselves and the campus from local, national, and international affairs, and when they found no student organization that embodied a similar commitment, they organized their own.

Traditionally, the *Daily Cardinal* was the most important student activity on campus. The paper reached and probably influenced more students than any other single organization and reflected the opinions of its readers more accurately than most regular newspapers do. Veteran domination of the *Daily Cardinal* in the postwar years, therefore, was a measure of veteran interest in student activities as well as a commentary of veteran attitudes and values. From April 1945 to April 1949 the editors of the paper were veterans, as were most of the staff workers who performed the routine tasks.

In the editorials, columns, and news stories published by veterans ran a heavy concern for national and international affairs. British socialism, the United Nations, and the Greek civil war repeatedly dominated the front page. Editorials stated the paper's position on the Tennessee Valley Authority, the farm-subsidy program, and the Taft-Hartley Act. A regular column, "Covering the Legislature," helped keep students abreast of state politics, and during 1946–1947 the paper featured Herblock's daily cartoons. Campus conditions under fire from the paper included "mass-production education," commercialism in collegiate athletics, and infringement of academic freedom.

The writings of Karl E. Meyer, the first nonveteran editor in the postwar era, reveal both the character of the paper under veteran leadership and the respect Meyer felt for the veterans. He praised veterans for their "dissatisfaction with the status quo" and for their "real concern for basic problems of student and national welfare." In January 1951 Meyer declared that "only three years ago the whole atmosphere of the campus was entirely different—and better," and then he paid tribute to "the last of the hell-raising veterans who once made this University a stimulating and lively place for an all-too-brief post-war period." Meyer's analysis found supporters but no dissenters.[38]

The extent and character of veteran participation in extracurricular activities combined with veteran academic accomplishment to produce a distinguished record. The most important, and perhaps the most remarkable, characteristic of the generation which established that record was the ability to adjust to civilian life, to academic life, to crowded classrooms, to inadequate housing, and to close integration with younger persons without military experience. Although the reasons for this ease of adjustment cannot be precisely measured, some observations are possible. First, there were too many veterans to create an adjustment problem. For three years (1946–1949) veterans constituted a majority of all students and an overwhelming majority of male students (82 percent in September 1946); they dominated the university and inadvertently forced the nonveteran student to make any needed adjustment. Second, most persons overemphasized the veteran adjustment problem. The veteran returned to a life he had known for at least eighteen years and for which he now had deeper respect and longing. In most cases the more severe adjustment had been the change from civilian to soldier. Third, the university administration clearly worked hard to accommodate veterans and thus allayed potential trouble. In this endeavor the administration benefited from the university's tradition of open debate, nonconformity, and academic superiority.[39] Fourth, in spite of the shortages, the inflation, and the uncertainty of world affairs during the immediate postwar years, veterans realized the advantage of attending the university, especially when they compared their student status with their teenage years during the depression, and their coming of age during years of war. And fifth, the university provided an ideal way-station between service and civilian life. The impersonal aspects of a large university, the lines for food, books, and amusements, the communal living accommodations (some actually in military buildings), and the financial dependency upon the federal government all reminded the veteran of his military experience. Many of the campus buildings—Quonset-hut reading room, prefab classrooms—the opportunity for bull sessions, the convenient system to gripe against, and the acceptable wardrobe of flight jacket, khakis, and army shoes all reinforced the former associations.

In addition to the example of their superior performances, the veterans left a heritage to the college generations that followed. They made the married student an accepted part of academic life and demonstrated the feasibility of a massive federal-aid program to higher education. Veteran enrollment and demands also helped to increase state financial support of the university. Because veterans demanded no structural change in the university's administration, organization, or academic process their influence and importance remains in their performance, and such an influence is always more ephemeral than lasting. The World War II veterans who returned to the university a quarter of a century ago wanted to be treated first as students and then as veterans, and they wanted to be absorbed into the university with as little disruption as possible. They succeeded.

6. Thereafter

In education, however, the G.I. Bill carried the principle of demo-cratization too far.

> Seymour E. Harris, Harvard Professor, December 1947.

Only three years ago the whole atmosphere of the campus was entirely different—and better. . . . Veterans . . . once made this University a stimulating and lively place for an all-too-brief post-war period.

> Karl E. Meyer, Editor of The University of Wisconsin *Daily Cardinal*, January 1951.

The Department of Defense does not favor legislation which provides the serviceman with an inducement to leave military service after accruing entitlement to education or training benefits under such legislation.

> William W. Berg, General, U.S. Air Force, September 1965.

By far the most farsighted veterans' program in our history was the original World War II G.I. Bill of 1944.

> Ralph Yarborough, U.S. Senator, September 1965.

THE ACCOMPLISHMENTS, intentional and unintentional, tangible and intangible, of the G.I. Bill's college program varied. The program fulfilled the objectives of the persons who initiated, designed, supported, and passed the legislation, but it also produced results totally unexpected in 1944. Veteran enrollment statistics documented the popularity of the college program and veteran academic records demonstrated its success. And the college program drew lavish praise, although congressional committees, journalists, and the public criticized the operation of various other parts of the G.I. Bill. By winning unusual support and a minimum of criticism from all segments of society the college program joined the Civilian Conservation Corps of the 1930s as probably the most widely admired and least criticized federal programs of their respective eras. This in itself was quite an accomplishment.

The persons responsible for the G.I. Bill and its college program exhibited a motivation more negative than positive. Recalling the events of the 1930s, they envisioned a postwar economy with substantial unemployment. And, logically, with a military force that counted fifteen million persons in 1944, they concluded that among the unemployed would be millions of veterans. Unemployed veterans, they remembered, had led a march on the nation's capitol in 1932 and had contributed to political instability in Europe throughout the 1920s and 1930s. The primary objective of the Servicemen's Readjustment Act of 1944, therefore, was to lessen the possibility of veteran unemployment and veteran discontent. Even the American Legion, which championed the G.I. Bill as a reward for the veteran, justified much of its position by reminding the nation that it would have chaos if the veterans felt mistreated. The college benefits, like other benefits, were means or programs designed to adjust the veteran into the American economy. In light of this central objective, then, the G.I. Bill proved an unqualified success. Through its titles Congress poured into the economy 14.5 billion dollars, 5.5 of them through the higher education provisions. This economic and psychological stimulus played an important though immeasurable role in the economic prosperity of the first postwar decade. The veterans found jobs, and because the majority took training under one of the several provisions of the G.I. Bill, most found better jobs than they had held before the war or expected to hold after the war. Equally vital, the G.I. Bill combined with the prosperity to allay potential veteran discontent. Compared to American veterans of previous wars and compared to other groups in society, the World War II veterans were and have been singularly satisfied.

A secondary objective of the G.I. Bill was to replenish the supply of college graduates lost to the war, directly by battle deaths and indirectly by the inability of young men to enroll in college. The two executive committees, The Conference on Post-War Adjustment of Civilian and Military Personnel and The Armed Forces Committee on Postwar Educational Opportunities for Service Personnel, even discussed limiting educational benefits to veterans who wanted to pursue study in fields where manpower shortages existed. Neither Roosevelt, Congress, nor the American Legion supported this position. In fact, outside the two executive committees, no one evaluated the merits of the idea. Roosevelt lacked the time and Congress and the Legion usually rejected any idea that suggested economic planning.[1]

During 1943 and 1944 Congress believed that the postwar economy needed federal funds, but that the funds should have no strings attached. Give money to the veterans, the logic went. They would be satisfied and it would boost the economy. Beyond the grant, Congress was willing to leave the rest to the law of supply and demand. The implied faith was that veterans would naturally enter the professions with the greatest employment opportunities. In this secondary objective, to increase the number of college-trained persons, the G.I. Bill proved successful. Also, because of the act about 450,000 veterans attended college who otherwise would not have done so. But Congress, primarily concerned with the questions of unemployment and of potentially malcontented veterans, never even suggested an ideal number of veterans it wanted to entice onto college campuses. There was no gauge, therefore, upon which to measure the degree of success.

Because Congress, when it wrote the G.I. Bill, regarded higher education as a tool or device to help ward off a potential danger, it set or implied no educational objectives other than the vague desire to increase the number of college graduates, and it gave no thought to the impact the act would have upon college education. Hence, any effect the G.I. Bill had upon higher education was unintentional.

The G.I. Bill, of course, affected the colleges in several significant ways. When veterans brought their wives to a campus and administrators worked to provide living quarters for them, it marked both an official acceptance of and an encouragement to married students. This represented a complete departure from prewar policy, when many colleges automatically expelled any student who married. The example of the World War II veterans, the Korean G.I. Bill, the economic prosperity, and the steadily lowering marriage age permanently imbedded in higher education the concept of the married student. Throughout the 1950s, the open acknowledgment of this concept appeared on campuses across the country as school after school built modern brick apartments to replace the World War II veteran trailers and prefabs. For a girl, marriage and even children no longer meant the end of her college education. Low-cost housing, public acceptance, and the example of veterans permitted a student to combine marriage and graduate school far more easily than his prewar predecessor. Countless young couples started married life in a new social environment. Differences existed between starting married life in a noncampus environment and in a campus atmosphere. In the latter, a couple usually had more married friends of the same age, values, and interests, all living in surroundings less financially competitive and less materialistic than society as a whole. The move away from the married-student culture, therefore, often created an adjustment problem.

Even more intangible than the influence of married students was the G.I. Bill's impact on the growth of colleges. Following World War II the nation's colleges strained their facilities and accommodated a total enrollment seventy-five percent greater than their prewar record. In the process many schools doubled their earlier enrollments. Despite crowded conditions, veterans, educators, and the public hailed the G.I. Bill's college program as an overwhelming success. During the middle and late 1950s, when educators and state legislatures planned for the enrollment deluge of the 1960s, they recalled the manner in which colleges responded to the veteran enrollment.

Larger classes, larger colleges, and increased use of graduate students as teachers had accomplished educational wonders for the veterans, who seemed grateful. The uncritical acceptance of largeness became a major legacy of the G.I. Bill. This legacy, in turn, served as perhaps the most important intellectual foundation for bigness that characterized higher education during the 1960s and 1970s. To meet the increased enrollment demands educators and legislators relied heavily upon larger and larger schools. In 1948, the peak of the postwar years, there were eight universities with over 20,000 students; in 1967 there were fifty-five. During the same period more than sixty universities pushed their enrollments past the 10,000 mark for the first time. The administrators who directed the postwar increases, however, did so in the belief that the expansion was a temporary situation.[2]

The persons who made the decisions to establish huge enrollments as a permanent condition either misread or forgot the veteran experience of 1945 to 1950, although many of these decision makers had studied under the G.I. Bill. World War II veterans tolerated, but did not embrace, large classes and large enrollments. Various veterans complained about the "assembly line operations in the classroom," the "atmosphere resembling the production line of a Detroit foundry," and the increased pressure "to make education an impersonal, mass affair." [3] Most veterans undoubtedly agreed with John Higham, a history graduate student at the University of Wisconsin, when he declared in 1947 that "the colleges admittedly have done a commendable job in absorbing the veteran flood, but only their most zealous apologists would argue that the overworked and overrun institutions of today provide as good an education as those of yesterday." [4]

There were several reasons why veterans, while aware of short-comings, quietly accepted their academic situation. They realized that the colleges were doing all they could and that there just was no alternative. No one had expected the overwhelming veteran response to the G.I. Bill, and even if he had there was neither time, nor labor, nor building materials available to construct new buildings. Nor were there enough professors. Too, military experience had helped condition the veterans to tolerate bigness, standing in lines, and improvisation. Stanford University undergraduate, Cecil F. Rospaw, who like Higham had attended college before the war, voiced a common sentiment when he wrote that "nothing can be done about the size of classes or the drop in quality of the instructors." [5] Nonveteran students, meanwhile, remained almost subdued, feeling somewhat awed in the presence of veteran classmates. They were, moreover, thankful to be registered, because most colleges gave veterans priority of admissions.

Rather than protesting against conditions that could not be changed, or against college administrators who were doing "a commendable job," veterans and nonveterans alike accepted their situation with resignation and dignity. They were a grateful college generation, the twenty percent who could not have attended without the G.I. Bill, the other eighty percent who enjoyed the financial assistance, and the countless thousands happy to have survived the war. Veteran acceptance of large enrollments, then, was a tribute to their understanding and character.

The World War II G.I. Bill also inspired and shaped two later G.I. Bills, the Korean and the Vietnamese. "Within approximately 2 weeks after the start of the Korean conflict on June 27, 1950," John Rankin, chairman of the House Committee on Veterans' Affairs, started the legislative machinery to extend the benefits of "the Servicemen's Readjustment Act of 1944 to the veterans of the Korean conflict." [6] Two years later the Senate, by voice vote, and the House by a 361 to 1 vote, approved the Veterans' Readjustment Assistance Act of

1952, also known as Public Law 550. Veterans who served between 27 June 1950 and 31 January 1955 received unemployment insurance, job placement, home loans, and mustering-out pay benefits similar to those offered in the 1944 act. In general, the educational and training provisions paralleled the earlier act; Congress, however, did make important modifications. Whereas the World War II Act awarded all veterans a year of training plus an additional day of training or education for each day served, the Korean Act dropped the automatic first year and instead awarded a day and a half of training for each day served. This change worked against the person who served less than two years. More importantly, the 1952 act allowed a maximum of thirty-six months of training, in contrast to the earlier act's four years. Also, the 1952 act included no payment to the colleges for tuition, books, and fees, compared to the $500 allotted in the 1944 legislation. Monthly subsistence payments under the Korean Act were higher than they had been for World War II veterans, $110, $135, and $160 versus $75, $105, and $120. The increase, however, noticeably and intentionally failed to offset the abolition of the $500 tuition payment and a higher cost of living. From his monthly check the Korean veteran had to pay all his college expenses, tuition, fees, books, and subsistence.

The new type of payment and new formula for determining the number of days of eligibility stemmed from the experience administrators gained from their work with the 1944 act. Before Congress passed the Korean G.I. Bill it weighed the findings of several investigations of the operation of the World War II Act. During 1950, 1951, and early 1952, the Veterans' Administration, the General Accounting Office, and a special House committee all investigated education and training under the World War II Bill and reported their findings.[7] Before Congress took final action both the Senate Committee on Labor and Public Welfare and the House Committee on Veterans' Affairs conducted hearings.[8] The latter committee also held a series of informal round-table conferences with officials of the V.A., U.S. Office of Education, and other federal agencies involved with the operation of the G.I. Bill.

Of all the investigations and hearings, the most influential proved to be the House Select Committee to Investigate Educational Programs under the G.I. Bill. Headed by Texas Democrat, Olin E. Teague, the committee spent eighteen months on its study and solicited the cooperation of federal agencies, veteran organizations, education associations, and individuals. The committee submitted its report to the House in February 1952 and five months later saw its recommendations become the educational provisions of the Korean G.I. Bill. In its final report the committee did not use the fear of depression and veteran discontent to justify the legislation. The prosperity and veteran contentment of the postwar years had frightened away the ghosts of the 1930s who had haunted those responsible for the 1944 G.I. Bill.

In addition to the changed economic conditions, there were at least two other reasons why the Korean Act differed from the World War II Act. First, although the V.A. and various congressional committees praised the college portion of the G.I. Bill, they found that administrative problems and abuses had developed over tuition, book, and fees payments. College officials agreed that tuition payment was a problem and they universally disliked the responsibility involved with payment for veterans' books, fees, and supplies. The decision to abolish these payments and to combine all benefits into a single monthly check to the veteran, therefore, stemmed directly from the operation of the World War II G.I. Bill.

A second motive, which helped shape the Korean Bill in general and which specifically determined lower financial benefits, was the belief within the academic community that the World War II G.I. Bill had been too generous. The Association of Land-Grant Colleges and Universities, for example, believed that because the country confronted "a situation entirely different from what it faced at the end of World War II, it . . . [was] time to adopt a new approach." Military service, the association declared, was a duty and "when it is universal no reward should be expected or given." But the association recognized that conscription lessened the possibility that "young people with ability but without money" would attend college, and that the country could not "afford this loss."

To offset this intolerable possibility, the association formally recommended a program "in the national interest, and not in the selfish interest of either institutions or individuals." The program should pay "$800 to $900" a year to a veteran whose education had been "substantially interrupted by military service." [9] Payment, the association suggested further, "should not cover the full cost of education or be differentiated as to dependency." The Teague Committee Report commented that the program of the Association of Land-Grant Colleges and Universities was "typical in most respects of other recommendations which have been received from college groups and college administrators." College administrators and college organizations, the Teague Report continued, "have been consistent" in their view that "the amount of aid provided under the World War II program has been sufficiently large to stimulate many veterans to go to school for the purpose of securing subsistence payments, rather than a primary interest in education." [10]

The House Committee on Veterans' Affairs accepted the Teague Report and incorporated its recommendations into the Korean G.I. Bill. In its final report the Veterans' Affairs Committee emphasized "that it is not the intention of this legislation to establish a program which completely subsidizes the cost of a veteran's education." [11] With colleges asking for lower benefit payments, with a healthy economy, with no veteran unrest or veteran pressure comparable to the pressure the American Legion applied during 1943 and 1944, Congress drafted the Korean G.I. Bill less generously than its World War II parent.[12] Nevertheless, Congress provided educational benefits that exceeded what colleges deemed necessary or desirable.

On 3 March 1966, when it passed the Veterans' Readjustment Benefits Act of 1966, Congress gave birth to the grandchild of the World War II G.I. Bill. The 1966 act, like its ancestors of 1944 and 1952, reflected conditions within society at the time of enactment. For the Vietnam era veteran (service after 31 January 1955), this meant less generous education benefits. Whereas the Korean bill extended benefits to a person with 90 days of service, the Vietnam bill required 180 days; whereas the 1952 act awarded a day and a half training for each day served, the 1966 act granted a day of training; and whereas the Korean act paid monthly allowances of $110, $135, and $160, the Vietnam act paid amounts of $100, $125, and $150. In 1970 the Vietnam allowances increased to $175, $205, and $230, and in 1972 increased again to $220, $261, and $298. Both increases included additional allowances for each dependent beyond the first two.

To support their calls for a third G.I. Bill, the American Legion, congressional leaders, the V.A., and other organizations repeatedly cited the success of the World War II and Korean Bills. The AFL-CIO, for example, reminded the House Committee on Veterans' Affairs that the first two bills increased "the standard of living of the veterans and their families," raised "the levels of education and skills of the Nation," and proved "an exceptionally wise investment." Senator Ralph Yarborough, Texas Democrat, who led the unsuccessful campaign for a Cold War G.I. Bill and then worked for the Vietnam G.I. Bill, called the World War II act" one of the most beneficial, far-reaching programs ever instituted in American life." Like the AFL-CIO, Yarborough pointed out that the veterans who utilized the G.I. Bill paid higher taxes than nonveterans or veterans who failed to use the benefits. The larger tax payments, Yarborough reasoned, more than repaid what the program cost.[13] In 1965 Cyril F. Brickfield, the V.A.'s Deputy Administrator of Veterans' Affairs, publicly agreed. He published an article reporting the V.A.'s conclusions that the G.I. Bill already had repaid its initial cost, and that the G.I. Bill "was one of the most successful pieces of legislation ever enacted." [14]

Despite the obvious favorable results of the World War II and Korean Bills, Congress made the provisions of the Vietnam G.I. Bill more limited than the earlier acts. There were several reasons. The economy was stronger in 1966 than it had been in 1944 and 1952. The V.A., for example, rationalized more stringent benefits because of the greater educational opportunities within the military services, the increased availability of government educational loans and scholarships, and the healthier economy.[15] Also, the Department of Defense opposed "legislation which provides the serviceman with an inducement to leave the military service after accruing entitlement to educational or training benefits under such legislation." [16] In 1966, moreover, the magnitude of the war in Vietnam had not yet reached the proportions of the Korean conflict. And, of course, an influential, vocal, and growing segment of the American public opposed the war and disapproved of the military who fought it.

Obviously, the World War II act served as the model for the Korean and Vietnam G.I. Bills. Also, by the timing and character of its action, Congress clearly indicated that in an era of cold war, limited hot wars, and heavy defense spending, it would support a G.I. Bill only when there were sustained casualty lists. The two most important organizations involved with veteran benefits, the V.A. and the American Legion explicitly expressed the same sentiment. While both organizations opposed a "Cold War G.I. Bill" between 1955 and 1965, they supported similar legislation "with the escalation of hostilities in Vietnam." [17] The generosity of the benefits contained in the 1952 and 1966 acts, of course, reflected conditions during their years of passage. And finally, despite the enduring legislative similarities of the three G.I. Bills, the prime concern of the men who nurtured them differed. In 1944 the prime motivating force was the economy, while in 1952 and 1966 the idea was to reward veterans.

In addition to fulfilling its objectives, encouraging student marriages, promoting larger colleges, and inspiring two other G.I. Bills, the Servicemen's Readjustment Act of 1944 prompted establishment of a Presidential Commission on Higher Education. On 13 July 1946, President Truman, acting upon the proposal of John Snyder, Director of War Mobilization and Reconversion, appointed a commission to "reexamine our system of higher education in terms of its objectives, methods, and facilities; and in the light of the social role it has to play." Truman explained to the members of the commission why he wanted such a reexamination. The veterans, he wrote, were taxing the resources and resourcefulness of the nation's colleges. Composed of twenty-eight prominent persons and chaired by George F. Zook, president of the American Council on Education, the commission presented its report to Truman in December 1948. Published under the general title *Higher Education for American Democracy*, the report consisted of six small volumes dealing with goals, opportunity, organization, faculty, and financing.[18]

The commission made bold recommendations. It proposed that the nation "make education through the fourteenth grade available in the same way that high school education is now available," and that the federal government, "following broadly the precedent set by the G.I. Bill," establish a massive program of grants-in-aid to undergraduates and fellowships to graduate students. The commission's objective was to remove the economic barriers to higher education.[19] Although the report stirred a lively debate among educators, it had little measurable effect upon higher education.[20] Congress failed to establish the huge grant and fellowship program the commission wanted. Higher education did move in the direction the commission recommended, but the demands of national defense, of consumers, and of rising social aspirations were the prime instigators of this movement.

Because G.I. Bill veterans completely dominated higher education between 1945 and 1950 and because they were so distinctive in age, numbers, and achievement, many later observers, including historians and educators, attributed to them and to the G.I. Bill unwarranted powers. The G.I. Bill veterans were older, better students, and more highly motivated. Their maturity raised academic and moral standards, and they set the pattern of campus behavior for over half a decade. They included a number of academic late-bloomers and an increased percentage of students from the lower social and economic levels of society. But in general background, attitudes toward college and society, courses of study, and even disposition of time, veterans and nonveterans possessed striking similarities and only slight differences. Of the "450,000 engineers, 180,000 doctors, dentists, and nurses, 360,000 school teachers, 150,000 scientists, 243,000 accountants, 107,000 lawyers, [and] 36,000 clergymen" who earned degrees under provisions of the G.I. Bill, at least eighty percent would have done so without the legislation.[21]

Nor did the G.I. Bill's college program fundamentally alter the structure of higher education, except, of course, to encourage bigness. In terms of admission, administration, curriculum, financing, and instruction, American colleges in 1950 resembled closely their prewar establishments. Between 1945 and 1950 colleges simply were too busy to study and restructure themselves, and so they functioned much the same as they had before the war. During the 1950s and early 1960s several important trends in higher education—the mushroomed research activities, the rise in status of technical and science departments, the increased prestige of university professors, and the growth of graduate education—developed from the demands of the Defense Department and from a technological, consumption-oriented society, not from the influence of the G.I. Bill. In 1958, for example, Congress passed the impressive National Defense Education Act as a direct reaction to the Soviet Union's launching of the earth's first man-made satellite. The G.I. Bill, by providing an excellent example to the contrary eased fears that massive federal aid to education invariably meant federal control. In this indirect fashion it has contributed to the various federal programs of the past two decades. But the fear of federal control of education continued, kept alive and strong by the opponents of federal attempts to desegregate schools and to improve educational opportunities for minority groups.

The G.I. Bill's success provided evidence that could be used to justify bold action. Veterans showed that increased government support of education, especially for minority groups who required assistance, was an investment which paid rich dividends to society and to the concept of democracy. The G.I. Bill also proved that a substantial portion of the nation's youth had the ability but not the money to enter college. Despite the G.I. Bill experience and the President's Commission on Higher Education, the country failed to move forward with the speed and commitment that many educators felt desirable. The 1970 report of the Carnegie Commission on Higher Education testified as to how far the country had to travel before ability and not financial resources became the test of admission to college. By the year 2000, the report, if adopted, would guarantee every American equal opportunity to attend college.

The recurring gaps between expectations and realizations that developed from both the conception and operation of the G.I. Bill revealed the fallibility of conventional wisdom. Designed to operate during economic depression, the act instead functioned in an era of prosperity. Veteran and public acceptance of the act, moreover, transformed the basic intent of Congress. Educators and government officials consistently and drastically underestimated the numbers of veterans who would take advantage of the act's benefits and enroll at college. These same educators and government officials firmly believed that, for all practical purposes, veterans who were married, or over twenty-five years old, or out of school several years would not become college students upon their return to civilian life. In practice veterans in all three categories flocked to college, with half of all veteran students married. The majority of educators, government officials, and public commentators, likewise, were apprehensive about the ability of veterans to adjust, academically and socially, to college. Once enrolled, veterans quickly exposed the inaccuracy of such apprehensions. Indeed, the most consistent theme in the story of the G.I. Bill was the element of the unexpected.

Perhaps the most astounding incident associated with the G.I. Bill, once it had demonstrated its overwhelming success, took place when the Teague Committee investigated the World War II act preparatory to congressional enactment of the Korean G.I. Bill. Despite the almost unanimous conclusions of studies that documented the superiority of veteran over nonveteran academic achievement, the nation's "college groups and college administrators" consistently felt that "many veterans" had enrolled in college "for the purpose of securing subsistence payments, rather than a primary interest in education," and for this reason the academic community favored less generous benefits for the Korean veteran.[22]

In retrospect, the G.I. Bill veterans acted predictably. Americans always have placed high value on education as the means to social and economic advancement. In one way, the G.I. Bill's education title was a product of that value.[23] The relationship between employment and education during the 1930s and between military rank and education during the war years combined with this traditional American value to spur men to college. Once on campus veterans found themselves the majority of male students, set the academic and social milieu, and forced nonveteran males to make any needed adjustment to the new atmosphere. Society, meanwhile, treated veterans as heroes and colleges gave them top priority in every area. For veterans, college served as a convenient way station between military and civilian life. And, of course, the G.I. Bill was not coercive. Veterans who became dissatisfied could drop out at any time. With so many advantages and few obstacles, the veterans easily made the G.I. Bill a success. The surprising aspect about the Bill was not its success, but the fact that so few people in 1944 and 1945 recognized its potential.

Bibliographical Note

The sources used in writing this book vary from chapter to chapter. Manuscript collections and Congressional hearings constitute the primary research basis for chapter one, "Origins and Motives." The records of the National Resources Planning Board, housed in the National Archives, includes minutes of meetings, reports, pamphlets, and letters of the "Conference on Post-war Readjustment of Civilian and Military Personnel," as well as useful manuscripts relating to activities of the Board. The Franklin D. Roosevelt Papers in Hyde Park, New York, contain three indispensable files for understanding the origins of the G.I. Bill: "Armed Forces Committee on Postwar Educational Opportunities for Service Personnel" (Official file 5182); "G.I. Bill of Rights" (Official file 4675–R); and "National Resources Planning Board" (Official file 1092). Also useful are "Post War Problems" (Official file 4351), "1945" (Official file 1571–A), "Miscellaneous (1944–1945)" (Official file 227), and "Veterans Administration" (Official file 8). Among the Papers of Samuel I. Rosenman is the important "War Veterans Legislation" (File 6D–13). The American Legion maintains excellent archives in its National Headquarters. Its files, "Great-War—G.I. Bill," are rich in detail, include material up to the present day, and are readily accessible. The Congressional hearings on the G.I. Bill proposal—House Committee on World War Veterans' Legislation (78th Cong., 2d sess.), Senate Committee on Finance (78th Cong., 2d sess.), and Senate Committee on Education and Labor (78th Cong., 1st sess.)—provide a broad spectrum of opinion from politicians, officials of veteran organizations, and educators.

Unlike chapter one, which focuses upon a specific proposal and the organizations and persons responsible for its conception and legislative birth, chapter two, "Anticipation and Reaction," describes a national attitude in general and the attitude of educators in particular. Also, the chapter summarizes the actions colleges took preparing for veteran students. Most of the chapter, therefore, is based upon a wide range of contemporary books and journal articles. The most useful journals reporting both the attitude of educators and the activities of colleges are *School and Society*, published weekly for the Society for the Advancement of Education, Inc., *Journal of Higher Education*, published by Ohio State University, and *Higher Education*, published semimonthly by the Higher Education Division of the U.S. Office of Education. For samplings of what colleges did to prepare for veterans see Francis J. Brown, *Educational Opportunities for Veterans* (Washington: Public Affairs Press, 1946); E. F. Linquist, "The Use of Tests in the Accreditation of Military Experience and in the Educational Placement of War Veterans," *Education Record* 25 (October 1944): 357–76; Byron H. Atkinson and Robert W. Webb, "Refresher Courses for Veterans," *Journal of Higher Education* 17 (October 1946): 377–80; and James D. Kline, "Specialized Counseling for Veterans at the University of Minnesota," *Educational Outlook* 22 (November 1947): 22–26. Typical of the many books about veterans are Willard Waller, *The Veteran Comes Back* (New York: The Dryden Press, 1944), Dixon Wector, *When Johnny Comes Marching Home* (Boston: Houghton Mifflin, 1944), and Charles G. Bolte, *The New Veteran* (New York: Reynal and Hitchcock, 1945). For a thoughtful summary of higher education in 1945 see Benjamin Fine, *Democratic Education* (New York: Thomas Y. Crowell, 1945). The "World War II G.I. Bill File," part of the Harry S. Truman Papers, in Independence, Missouri, is disappointing but does supplement the Congressional hearings, journals, and Legion files from which I wrote the last section (dealing with the G.I. Bill amendments of December 1945) of this chapter.

For chapter three, "The Pleasant Surprise," which describes veteran enrollment and academic performance, the major sources include records from the Vocational Rehabilitation and Education Division of the Veterans Administration, Washington, D.C.; the results of numerous case studies of veterans published in journals; the essential statistical volume, Norman Frederiksen and William B. Schrader, *Adjustment to College* (Princeton: Educational Testing Service, 1951); and several of Benjamin Fine's surveys for the *New York Times*. The most valuable V.A. records were the "Consolidated Monthly Reports," the file "Readjustment Training (P.L. 346)," and several Information Bulletins. Examples of the pertinent articles are Byron H. Atkinson, "Veteran vs Non-Veteran Performance at UCLA," *Journal of Educational Research* 43 (December 1949): 299–302; Ronald B. Thompson and S. L. Pressey, "Analysis of the Academic Records of 2,144 Veterans," *College and University* 23 (January 1948): 242–52; and Clark Tibbitts and Woodrow W. Hunter, "Veterans and Non-Veterans at the University of Michigan," *School and Society* 65 (10 May 1947): 347–50.

Chapter four, "Administration," examines the V.A., Congress, colleges, and veterans from an administrative perspective. Several reports and Congressional hearings provide the basis of my discussion of the V.A. and much of Congress's role in the administration of the G.I. Bill. See *Report of the House Select Committee to Investigate Educational and Training Programs under G.I. Bill* (81st Cong., 2d sess.), *Management Survey of Activities of the Veterans Administration by the Firm of Booz-Allen-Hamilton* (82d Cong., 2d sess.), *The President's Commission on Veterans' Pensions, A Report on Veterans' Benefits in the United States, Staff Report IX, Part B: Readjustment Benefits: Education and Training, and Employment and Unemployment* (84th Cong., 2d sess.), and *General Accounting Office Report of Survey-Veterans' Education and Training Program* (82d Cong., 1st sess.). Also see *House Report No. 1375* (82d Cong., 2d sess.) and *Senate Report No. 420* (80th Cong., 1st sess.). The most useful hearings are House Committee on Veterans Affairs (80th Cong., 1st sess.; and 82d Cong., 2d sess.) and Senate Committee on Labor and Public Welfare (80th Cong., 1st sess.). The annual reports of the Federal Works Agency and the U.S. Housing and Home Finance Agency help explain Congress's attempt to ease the strain on colleges' physical plants. For the pages on New York State and the veteran see J. Hillis Miller and John S. Allen, *Veterans Challenge the Colleges* (New York: King's Crown Press, 1947) and Amy M. Gilbert, *Associated Colleges of Upper New York* (Ithaca: Cornell University Press, 1950). Numerous articles tell the stories of the veterans and the colleges. For examples, see Benjamin Fine, "College at Brown University for Veterans Without Credits Proves a Great Success," *New York Times,* 13 April 1947; Benjamin Quarles, "The Background of the 1947 College Student," *Quarterly Review of Higher Education Among Negroes* 15 (April 1947): 87–90; James A. Atkins, "Negro Educational Institutions and the Veterans' Educational Facilities Program," *Journal of Negro Education* 17 (Spring 1948): 141–53; and "Veterans at College," *Life* 22 (21 April 1947): 105–13.

Materials in the University of Wisconsin Archives, supplemented by the valuable office files of Veterans Counsellor Douglas A. Dixon, provide the research base for chapter five, "The University of Wisconsin: A Case Study." Among its manuscripts the Archives contains enrollment reports, housing records, a few items from the Office of Veterans Affairs, incomplete files of faculty committees, and papers of a few administrators. The Archives also holds copies of the printed presidential reports, University Bulletins, and the *Daily Cardinal.*

Reports of Congressional investigations of the G.I. Bill, Congressional hearings on legislation to enact two additional G.I. Bills, and miscellaneous articles serve as the foundation for my analysis in chapter six, "Thereafter." The reports are *House Report No. 1943* (82d Cong., 2d sess.), *House Report No. 3253* (81st Cong., 2d sess.), *House Report No. 1375* (82d Cong., 2d sess.), *House Committee Print No. 160* (82d Cong., 1st sess.), and *House Committee Print No. 210* (81st Cong., 2d sess.). For a discussion of attitudes toward a G.I. Bill for veterans of the Korean conflict see the hearings held by the Senate Committee on Labor and Public Welfare (82d Cong., 1st sess.) and the House Committee on Veterans' Affairs (82d Cong., 2d sess.). For a similar discussion concerning post-Korean veterans see the hearings by the House Committee on Veterans' Affairs (89th Cong., 1st sess., and 89th Cong., 2d sess.).

Throughout my research I found the *New York Times* valuable for its coverage of higher education and veterans, especially the excellent work of its education editor Benjamin Fine. I obtained statistics from a number of sources: the V.A., the U.S. Office of Education's *Biennial Surveys* and its *Circulars* on enrollment, Congressional reports, and the handy volume by Kenneth A. Simon and W. Vance Grant, *Digest of Educational Statistics 1968* (Washington: Government Printing Office, 1968).

Secondary works proved disappointing. Histories of individual colleges and universities that cover the post World War II era devote, at best, a few pages and no analysis to the G.I. Bill veterans. None of the histories of higher education even begin to discuss the G.I. Bill. Frederick Rudolph's superb *The American College and University* (New York: Alfred A. Knopf, 1968) does not mention it; John S. Brubacher and Willis Rudy, *Higher Education in Transition: An American History 1636–1956* (New York: Harper and Brothers, 1958) spend a paragraph on the topic; and William Clyde DeVance, *Higher Education in Twentieth-Century America* (Cambridge, Mass.: Harvard University Press, 1965) limits his discussion to ten sentences scattered on six different pages.

The one historian who has written about the G.I. Bill is Davis R. B. Ross. In his fine book, *Preparing for Ulysses: Politics and Veterans During World War II*, Ross spends a chapter on the legislative history of the Act. My first chapter includes a brief summary of the legislative history of the G.I. Bill but its main objectives were to examine the origin of the idea to send veterans to college, to analyze those portions of G.I. Bill proposals that dealt with higher education, and to discuss the motives of the persons and organizations responsible for The Servicemen's Readjustment Act of 1944.

In this "Note" I briefly summarized the major sources for each chapter. For a complete identification of sources, please see the footnotes.

Notes

CHAPTER 1

¹ In several ways, of course, the G.I. Bill represented a new dimension of veteran benefits, but the new dimension rested on old foundations. For the new dimension see U.S., Congress, House, *The President's Commission on Veterans' Pensions, A Report on Veterans' Benefits In The United States, Staff Report IX, Part A: Readjustment Benefits: General Survey and Appraisal*, 84th Cong., 2d sess., 1956, H. Print 289, p. 1. Davis R. B. Ross, *Preparing for Ulysses: Politics and Veterans during World War II* (New York: Columbia University Press, 1969), especially p. 4,290.

² Roosevelt's Message on the State of the Union, 11 January 1944, found in Samuel J. Rosenman ed., *The Public Papers and Addresses of Franklin D. Roosevelt* (New York: Harper and Brothers, 1950), 1944–1945 volume, pp. 41–42; Samuel I. Rosenman, *Working with Roosevelt* (New York: Harper and Brothers, 1952), pp. 414–16.

³ Roosevelt to Owen D. Young, box 5, official file 1092, National Resources Planning Board papers, Franklin D. Roosevelt Library, Hyde Park, New York.

⁴ Frederick A. Delano to Roosevelt, n.d., and Delano to Roosevelt, "Memorandum for the President," 12 February 1940, box 5, NRPB papers, Roosevelt Library.

⁵ Rosenman, *The Public Papers and Addresses of Franklin D. Roosevelt*, 1942 volume, p. 52.

⁶ Ibid., pp. 53–54. Two years later Roosevelt dramatized these principles in his 1944 "Message on the State of the Union" and asked Congress "to explore the means for implementing this economic bill of rights." Rosenman, *The Public Papers and Addresses of Franklin D. Roosevelt*, 1944–1945 volume, pp. 41–42.

⁷ Delano to Roosevelt, 1 July 1942, Roosevelt to Delano, 6 July 1942, box 10, NRPB papers, Roosevelt library. Ross credits Leonard Outhwaite, who drafted legislative proposals from his position within the Bureau of the Budget, as the prime mover behind Delano's suggestion. See Ross, *Preparing for Ulysses*, pp. 51–52.

⁸ The other members were Dr. Edward C. Elliott, Chief Professional and Technical Employment and Training Division, War Manpower Commission; Dr. William Haber, Director, Bureau of Program Requirements, War Manpower Commission; Major General Lewis B. Hershey, Director, Bureau of Selective Service, War Manpower Commission; Lieutenant Commander Ralph A. Sentman, U.S.N. (Ret.), Officer in Charge, Educational Services Section, Training Division, Bureau of Naval Personnel, Navy Department (who replaced Commander Burton Davis when Davis was ordered to sea); Howard R. Tolley, Chief, Bureau of Agricultural Economics, Department of Agriculture; Dr. Thomas J. Woofter, Jr., Director of Research, Federal Security Agency; and Leonard Outhwaite, NRPB, Secretary.

⁹ Three page agenda, titled "The Demobilization of Men, Program for Training, Counselling, Rehabilitation, Readjustment and Placement," file 830.31, Records of The National Resources Planning Board, Record Group 187, National Archives, Washington, D.C.. Hereafter cited as R.G. 187.

¹⁰ Minutes of the first meeting of the Post-war Manpower Conference (hereafter cited as PMC), 17 July 1942, and minutes of the fourth meeting, 27 August 1942, both file 830.31, R.G. 187.

¹¹ File 089, R.G. 187. George Sundborg, Senior Planning Technician, Region 10, NRPB, prepared the pamphlet.

¹² Files 455.3, 089, and 830.31, R.G. 187.

¹³ "Demobilization and Readjustment," file 830.31, R.G. 187, pp. 23, 75, 83, 87.

¹⁴ Ibid., pp. 37, 60.

¹⁵ Ibid., pp. 17, 70.

¹⁶ Roosevelt to Henry A. Wallace, 16 July 1943, file 830.31, R.G. 187. On 10 March

1943 Roosevelt submitted to Congress, along with "National Resources Development—Report for 1943," a second NRPB report, "Security, Work, and Relief Policies." The latter report, based upon a thorough study, recommended expanded government welfare programs, a permanent federal works program, increased government regulation of private industry, and a role in management for labor. Designed to prevent a postwar boom or depression and to guarantee every person a job, the report's recommendations raised the ire of conservatives. The public, on the other hand, responded with enthusiasm. Two public opinion surveys revealed that seventy-three percent of Americans supported the report's suggestion that the government guarantee a job for every worker, while eighty-three percent of Americans favored free medical care to all who needed but could not afford it. For the report and a discussion of it, see the *New York Times*, 11 March 1943, pp. 1, 12, 13. For the opinion polls, see 'Public Opinion and the NRPB Social Security Report," file 103.71, R.G. 187.

[17] Roosevelt to Delano, 6 July 1942, box 10, NRPB papers, Roosevelt Library; and minutes of the 8th meeting of the PMC, 5 November 1942, file 830.31, R.G. 187.

[18] Minutes of the 5th and 8th meetings of the PMC, 10 September 1942, and 5 November 1942; and Charles W. Elliott to Floyd W. Reeves, 20 January 1943, file 830.31, R.G. 187.

[19] Rosenman, *The Public Papers and Addresses of Franklin D. Roosevelt*, 1942 volume, p. 470.

[20] Roosevelt to Frederick H. Osborn, 19 November 1942, Papers of the Armed Forces Committee on Postwar Educational Opportunities for Service Personnel (hereafter cited as Osborn Committee papers), official file 5182, Roosevelt Library; also see Robert P. Patterson to Roosevelt, 12 November 1942, official file 5182, Roosevelt Papers, Roosevelt Library.

[21] Reeves to Charles Seymour, 8 January 1943; Reeves to Osborn, 8 January 1943; and Reeves to Thomas C. Blaisdell, Jr., 2 March 1943, file 825, R.G. 187.

[22] For a convenient comparison of the PMC and the Osborn Committee education plans, see "War Veterans Education," undated memorandum in folder "War Veterans Legislation," file 6D–13, papers of Samuel I. Rosenman, Roosevelt Library.

[23] U.S., Congress, House, *Post-War Educational Opportunities for Service Personnel*, 78th Cong., 1st sess., 1943, H. Document 344, pp. 6, 7, 9. For Osborn's views on the interrelationship of education and employment see his letter to Roosevelt, 20 September 1944, official file 5182, Roosevelt Library.

[24] Rosenman, *The Public Papers and Addresses of Franklin D. Roosevelt*, 1943 volume, pp. 333–35.

[25] Ross, *Preparing for Ulysses*, pp. 70–73.

[26] Roosevelt's Chief of Staff, General George C. Marshall, for example, while concerned about demobilized veterans believed that only members of Congress and the President, never the military, should take the initiative in drafting legislation.

[27] Oscar Cox to Harry Hopkins, 2 July 1943, box 3, Rosenman Papers, Roosevelt Library.

[28] For a parallel reconstruction of the PMC, the Osborn Committee reports, and Roosevelt's role in laying the ground work for the G.I. Bill, see Ross, *Preparing for Ulysses*, pp. 51–73, 92. My work, concentrating on higher education, has a different emphasis and focus than Ross and in several instances offers a different interpretation.

[29] Rosenman, *The Public Papers and Addresses of Franklin D. Roosevelt*, 1943 volume, pp. 450–51, 522–27.

[30] Reeves to Thomas E. Benner, 6 January 1943, Reeves to Mrs. Lewis S. Thompson, 15 May 1943, file 825, R.G. 187.

[31] See "Report of Subcommittee on Education," NRPB, 28 February 1942, file 830.31, R.G. 187.

[32] George F. Zook, "The President's Annual Report, 1942–1943" (7 May 1943), p. 49, American Council on Education Library, Washington, D.C.; ACE newsletter, *Higher Education and National Defense*, no. 55 (3 June 1943), pp. 8–9.

³³ U.S., Congress, Senate, Committee on Education and Labor, *Hearings on S. 1295 and S. 1509*, 78th Cong., 1st sess., 1943, p. 114. (hereafter cited as *Thomas Committee Hearings*).

³⁴ For the summary of the questionnaire, see *Higher Education and National Defense*, no. 57 (16 August 1943), ACE Library; for Zook's form letter to members of Congress, for the ACE plan, "A Proposed Program for War Service Education"; and for Zook to Rosenmann, 16 October 1943, see master speech files, 27 October 1943, papers of Franklin D. Roosevelt, Roosevelt Library. In contrast to the imprecise objective of the ACE plan, Zook did state in his letter to every member of Congress, 16 August 1943, that "in a very real sense the problem is, therefore, not only one of helping those young people whose education has been interrupted or shortened by service in the armed forces, but also one of national interest."

³⁵ Robert W. Sisson, Chairman of the Legion's National Rehabilitation Committee; Harry Colmery, past National Commander; Sam Rorex, a U.S. Attorney; W. B. Waldrip, a Detroit banker; R. M. McCurdy, vice chairman of the Legion's National Rehabilitation Committee and assistant city manager of Pasadena, California; Maurice F. Devine, chairman of the Legion's National Legislative Committee; and Lawrence J. Fenlon, chairman of the Legion's National Employment Committee.

³⁶ David Camelon, "I Saw the G.I. Bill Written: Part Two, A Surprise Attack," *The American Legion Magazine* 47 (October 1949): 52; Jack Cejnar to Charles N. Collatos, 27 November 1956, "Great War—Legion Bill," papers of the American Legion, folder 11, National Headquarters Library, Indianapolis, Indiana. Legion public-relations man, Stephen M. Walter, on the other hand, claimed that he "initiated it 'primarily' and was at least co-author." Ibid., Walter to Richard Seelye Jones, 17 December 1948, folder 10.

³⁷ *New York Times*, 25 March 1944, p. 3, reported that had all Senators been present, the vote would have been ninety six to zero; Senator Alben W. Barkley observed that "it is generally understood there is no one opposed to the bill." U.S., Congress, Senate, *Congressional Record*, 78th Cong., 2d sess., 1944, vol. 90, pt. 3: 3080.

³⁸ The topic of the month in the *Congressional Digest* 23 (March 1944): 65–96 was "Should the U.S. Office of Education Administer Funds for Post-War Education of Service Men and Women?"

³⁹ For an excellent account of the legislative and committee travels of the G.I. Bill, see Ross, *Preparing for Ulysses, chap. 4.*

⁴⁰ U.S., *Statutes at Large*, vol. 58, pt. 1: 288.

⁴¹ Atherton to Frederick E. Merritt, 8 November 1967, "Great War—Legion Bill," Legion Papers folder 12. When Atherton appeared before the Rankin Committee he expressed the same sentiment: U.S., Congress, House, Committee on World War Veterans' Legislation, *Hearings on H.R. 3817 and S. 1767*, 78th Cong., 2d sess., p. 24 (Hereafter cited as *Rankin Committee Hearings*).

⁴² *Rankin Committee Hearings*, 29 March 1944, p. 322; also see statement by Omar Ketchum, National Legislative Representative of the Veterans of Foreign Wars, in U.S., Congress, Senate, Committee on Finance, Subcommittee on Veterans' Legislation, *Hearings on Veterans' Omnibus Bill*, 78th Cong., 2d sess., 1944, p. 196 (hereafter cited as *Clark Committee Hearings*); and statement by Millard W. Rice, National Service Director, Disabled American Veterans, ibid., 24 January 1944, p. 78.

⁴³ Earlier the Roosevelt Administration had tentatively considered and rejected the idea of an omnibus bill. See Ross, *Preparing for Ulysses;* p. 98, 37n.

⁴⁴ *Clark Committee Hearings*, 14 January 1944, p. 20; also see Jack Cejnar to Steve Early, 19 May 1944, official file 4675-R, Roosevelt Papers.

⁴⁵ *New York Times*, 15 January 1944, p. 4.

⁴⁶ Milton Handler to Rosenman, 19 January 1944, file 6D-13, Rosenman Papers.

⁴⁷ Roosevelt, meanwhile, continued to work for a mustering-out-pay bill which he signed on 3 February 1944, and which constituted a presidential victory. Ross, *Preparing for Ulysses*, pp. 78–88.

⁴⁸ Rosenman, *The Public Papers and Addresses of Franklin D. Roosevelt*, 1944–1945 volume, p. 180.

⁴⁹ Ibid., p. 182.

⁵⁰ Ibid., 1933 volume, pp. 375–76, 1935 volume, p. 187.

⁵¹ *New York Times*, 21 July 1944, p. 8, 24 August 1944, p. 13; Rosenman to Roosevelt, 23 September 1944, official file 5182, Roosevelt Papers.

⁵² "Suggested Radio Interview" sent to every post commander (about 12,000 across the country), 11 January 1944, "Great War—Legion Bill," Legion Papers, folder 2.

⁵³ Statement of Harry W. Colmery, past commander of the Legion and member of the committee that wrote the bill, *Rankin Committee Hearings*, 30 March 1944, p. 396; David Camelon, "I Saw the G.I. Bill Written: Part One, The Fight for Mustering Out Pay," *The American Legion Magazine* 47 (September 1949): 47; Atherton, "Great War—Legion Bill," Legion Papers, folder 6; and *The National Legionnaire*, 10 (March 1944): 4.

⁵⁴ Quoted in the *New York Times*, 6 April 1942, p. 12.

⁵⁵ *New York Times*, 2 March 1944, p. 23.

⁵⁶ U.S., Congress, House, *Congressional Record*, 78th Cong., 2d sess., 1944, vol. 90, pt. 3: 4327.

⁵⁷ U.S., Congress, Senate, *Providing Federal Government Aid for the Readjustment in Civilian Life of Returning World War II Veterans, Senate Report 755—To Accompany S. 1767*, 78th Cong., 2d sess., 1944, p. 2.

⁵⁸ "Great War—Legion Bill," Legion Papers, folder 3.

⁵⁹ *Clark Committee Hearings*, 24 January 1944, p. 78; and 8 March 1944, p. 212.

⁶⁰ *Rankin Committee Hearings*, 17 January 1944, p. 99.

⁶¹ Ketchum declared on 12 January 1944 that the Legion bill, "almost without exception, . . . has long been the program of V. of F.W. adopted months ago in Convention." Ibid., p. 28; also see ibid., 18 January 1944, p. 127; 29 March 1944, p. 322; 30 March 1944, p. 396; and *Clark Committee Hearings*, 15 January 1944, pp. 38–39.

⁶² *New York Times*, 7 March 1944, p. 10.

⁶³ See *Clark Committee Hearings*, 11 February 1944, pp. 115–16, 121–33, and 138–41; Willard E. Givens, "Educational Legislation for Veterans," *Journal of the National Education Association* 33 (March 1944): 60; *New York Times*, 17 May 1944, p. 20; also see Givens before *Thomas Committee Hearings*, 14 December 1943, p. 87.

⁶⁴ *Thomas Committee Hearings*, 15 December 1943, p. 134.

⁶⁵ This fear of depression continued into the postwar period as well. At the end of 1946, *Fortune Magazine* polled the nation's top 15,000 business executives and reported that fifty-eight percent feared "an extended major depression with large-scale unemployment in the next ten years." Only twenty-eight percent of the executives believed the country could avoid a major depression. See "The Management Poll," *Fortune 35* (February 1947): 34; and John Kenneth Galbraith, *American Capitalism* (Boston: Houghton Mifflin Company, Sentry Edition, 1956), p. 66.

⁶⁶ In a minor way the G.I. Bill must also be seen as an attempt to head off a bonus for veterans, which had proved an unpleasant political issue during the 1920s and 1930s. The Clark Committee report (page 3) specifically states that "this bill will render unnecessary any consideration of adjusted compensation." Also see *New York Times*, 9 January 1944, p. 6; and 11 June 1944, p. 26.

⁶⁷ Samuel I. Rosenman, *Working With Roosevelt* (New York: Harper and Brothers, 1952), p. 394.

⁶⁸ Camelon, "I Saw the G.I. Bill Written: Part One, The Fight for Mustering Out Pay," p. 47; John Thomas Taylor to Arthur H. Clarke, 31 March 1948, and press release by National Commander Earle Cocke, Jr., 22 June 1951, "Great War—Legion Bill," Legion Papers, folder 10; National Commander Perry Brown, "Fellow Legionnaires," *The American Legion Magazine* 47 (1 August 1949): 10.

⁶⁹ Ross, *Preparing for Ulysses*, p. 283.

CHAPTER 2

¹ "The G.I. Bill of Rights," *New Republic* 111 (23 October, 1944):512; "Post-War Educational Plans of Soldiers," *Report no. B-133*, p. 10, Information and Education Division, Army Service Forces, March 1945. Hereafter cited as *Army Report no. B-133.*
² Willard Waller, *The Veteran Comes Back* (New York: The Dryden Press, 1944), pp. 292, 151, 158.
³ Charles G. Bolte, *The New Veteran* (New York: Reynal and Hitchcock, 1945), pp. 123-24.
⁴ For example, see Maxwell Droke, *Good-by to G.I.* (New York: Abingdon-Cokesbury Press, 1945), chap. 9; and Dorothy W. Baruch and Lee Edward Travis, *You're Out of the Service Now* (New York: Appleton-Century Company, Inc., 1946), chap. 9.
⁵ Morton Thompson, *How to Be a Civilian* (Garden City: Doubleday and Company, 1946); Irvin L. Child and Marjorie Van De Water, eds., *Psychology for the Returning Serviceman* (New York: Penguin Books, 1945).
⁶ Roosevelt to Byrnes, 4 August 1944, box 5, official file 4351, Roosevelt Papers.
⁷ "Soldiers' Attitudes Toward Post-War Education," *Education for Victory* 2 (3 March 1944): 1-2; *New York Times*, 3 January 1944, p. 8.
⁸ *Army Report no. B-133*, p. 10; Information and Education Division, Army Service Forces, "Soldiers' Plans For Full-Time School or College," *Report no. B-174*, 28 December 1945, title page and p. 1.
⁹ Typical of the single-campus polls were R.C.M. Flynt, "University of Colorado Polls Students in Service," *Higher Education* 1 (1 February 1945): 5-7; and Gertrude M. Hall, "Education Interests College G.I.'s," *School and Society* 61 (10 Feb. 1945): 94-96.
¹⁰ For example, see *New York Times*, 18 June 1944, IV, p. 9; "The G.I. Bill of Rights," *New Republic* 111 (23 October 1944): 512; Luther E. Woodward, "Adjustment Problems of Veterans," *Teachers College Record* 47 (October 1945): 18-19.
¹¹ Roosevelt to Frederick H. Osborn, 22 December 1944, official file 5182, Roosevelt Papers; Hines to Byrnes, 28 December 1944, official file 1571-A, Roosevelt Papers; Frank T. Hines, "Veterans and the Universities," *Journal of the American Association of Collegiate Registrars* 20 (January 1945): 175-83.
¹² Earl J. McGrath, "The Education of the Veteran," *Annals of the American Academy of Political and Social Science* 238 (March 1945): 84-85.
¹³ *New York Times*, 24 May 1945, p. 15.
¹⁴ Stanley Frank, "G.I.'s Reject Education," *Saturday Evening Post*, 18 August 1945, p. 20; also see Benjamin Fine, "Education in Review," *New York Times*, 13 January 1946, IV, p. 9.
¹⁵ The most notable exception was Floyd W. Reeves, who reported in December 1944 that the government had vastly underestimated the educational ambitions of servicemen. He predicted double the generally accepted projected enrollment and believed the student-veteran would spend years, not months, in school. *New York Times*, 11 December 1944, p. 23.
¹⁶ Benjamin Fine, *Democratic Education* (New York: Thomas Y. Crowell Company, 1945), p. 122; Frank T. Hines, "Education and Rehabilitation of Veterans with Special Reference to the Provisions of Public Laws 16 and 346," *Journal of Educational Sociology* 18 (October 1944): 75; Marshall R. Beard, "A College Administrator Speaks," *Social Education* 9 (March 1945): 106; Robert C. Woellner, "When Johnny Comes Marching Home," *School Review* 51 (December 1943): 577.
¹⁷ Dixon Wector, *When Johnny Comes Marching Home* (Boston: Houghton Mifflin Company, 1944), p. 558; Willard Waller, "Why Veterans Are Bitter," *American Mercury* 61 (August 1945): 147. Waller's book, *The Veteran Comes Back* (p. 13), concluded that "the veteran who comes home is a social problem, and certainly the major problem of the next few years." For support of Wector's position see Bolte, *The New Veteran*, p. 2; and Benjamin C. Bowker, *Out of Uniform* (New York: W. W. Norton and Company,

1946), p. xi. For support of Waller see George K. Pratt, *Soldier to Civilian* (New York: Whittlesey House, 1944), p. 7; and Muriel W. Brown, "When Our Servicemen Come Home," *Journal of Home Economics* 36 (December 1944): 626. Brown's article was the outcome of a conference attended by representatives from a number of organizations, including the Selective Service, the U.S. Office of Education, the National Committee for Mental Hygiene, and the Surgeon General's office of the U.S. Army.

¹⁸ For examples of this view see Henry C. Mills, "Adjusting the Veteran to Civilian College Life," *Educational Outlook* 19 (November 1944): 6–14; Joseph P. Blickensderfer, "The Universities and the Veteran: Whither?" *National Business Education Journal* 13 (December 1944): 25–27; S. H. Kraines, "Veteran and Postwar Education," *Journal of Higher Education* 16 (June 1945): 290–98; Walter Spearman and Jack R. Brown, "When the Veteran Goes to College," *South Atlantic Quarterly* 45 (January 1946): 31–42; Kimball Young, "What Kind of a Student Will the Veteran Be?" *Educational Record* 27 (April 1946): 168–77; H. H. Ranson, "Educational Plans of AAF Veterans," *Higher Education* 2 (5 May 1946): 8–9; N. M. McKnight, "They Know What They Want," *School and Society* 63 (29 June 1946): 449–52; and Walter R. Goetsch, "The G.I. in Civvies," *School and Society* 62 (21 July 1945): 45–46.

¹⁹ For examples of this view see Merl E. Bonney, "Some Psychological Effects of War on Soldiers," *Teachers College Journal* 15 (November 1943): 42–44; Morse A. Cartwright, "Marching Home," *Teachers College Record* 45 (April 1944): 437–51; Leland L. Medsker, "Problems Confronting Educational Institutions in Dealing with Veterans," *School Review* 54 (October 1946): 469–75; Alanson H. Edgerton, *Readjustment or Revolution?* (New York: McGraw-Hill, 1946); Pratt, *Soldier to Civilian:* Droke, *Good-by to G.I.;* Gabriel Frank, "Breadlines or Paylines," *Christian Science Monitor Magazine*, 15 September, 1945, p. 3; John Bergstresser, Louise Price, and Ruth G. Weintraub, "Community Living," *Journal of the National Association of Deans of Women* 8 (March 1945): 123–30; and *New York Times*, 4 March, 1944, p. 17.

²⁰ One survey "of 140 of the largest and most widely known American colleges and universities" revealed that "only four colleges" planned "to segregate veterans from other students." See Turus Hillway, "G.I. Joe and the Colleges," *Journal of Higher Education* 16 (June 1945): 285. Also see Carlos Baker, "From Hell to Helicon: A Prediction," *Saturday Review of Literature*, 17 March 1945, p. 13; Waller, *The Veteran Comes Back*, p. 154; and William Claflin, "Expectations of the Veteran," *Educational Outlook* 19 (November 1944): 5.

²¹ Edward C. McDonagh, "Some Hints to Professors," *American Association of University Professors Bulletin* 31 (Winter 1945): 643–47. In "Veteran Versus the Professor," *School and Society* 62 (1 September 1945): 132; Gaynor Pearson, a naval lieutenant, likewise suggested that "the teacher should also know, if time permits, the military record of every veteran in his classes." Army Doctor J. L. Rogers showed McDonagh's article "to be a number of patients and other servicemen who hope to be students soon" and reported "little" to criticize; see J. L. Rogers, "Additional Hints to Professors," *American Association of University Professors Bulletin* 32 (June 1946): 363–66.

²² Donald A. Stauffer, "Ex-Marine Returns to Teaching," *American Scholar* 15 (Winter 1945–1946): 28; Francis J. Brown, quoted in "The Veterans' Education Program," *School and Society* 60 (9 September 1944): 165.

²³ For example see "Two University Presidents on Critical Problems of Postwar Education," *School and Society* 61 (5 May 1945): 293–94; William E. Hays, "The Post-War Liberal Arts College and the G.I. Bill: An Analysis," *Education* 66 (September 1945): 47; "Post-War Education Needs Intelligent Planning and Directing," *Scientific American* 171 (August 1944): 75; *New York Times*, 11 June 1944, IV, p. 8.

²⁴ "Soldiers' Attitudes Toward Post-War Education," *Education for Victory* 2 (3 March 1944): 2; Willard Waller, "Which Veterans Should Go to College," *Ladies' Home Journal*, May 1945, pp. 143, 169; A. J. Brumbaugh, "Planning Education for Returning Members of the Armed Forces," American Association of Teachers Colleges, 23rd yearbook (1944), pp. 53–54.

²⁵ James B. Conant, "Annual Report of the President of the University," *Harvard Alumni Bulletin* 47 (3 February 1945): 286; ibid., 46 (22 January 1944): 244.

²⁶ Robert M. Hutchins, "The Threat to American Education," *Collier's*, 30 December 1944, pp. 20–21; also see "Bursars Rub Hands over G.I. Bill But College Standards May Suffer," *Newsweek*, 8 January 1945, pp. 66–69.

²⁷ *Higher Education and National Defense* 55 (3 June 1943): 1.

²⁸ For typical cases see R. H. Eckelberry, "The Veterans and the Colleges," *Journal of Higher Education* 15 (January 1944): 51–52; various articles in *Annals of the American Academy of Political and Social Sciences* 231 (January 1944); and Earl J. McGrath, "The College Program and the Returning Service Man," *Association of American Colleges Bulletin* 30 (March 1944): 21–31.

²⁹ *New York Times*, 6 March 1946, p. 33; ibid., 17 April 1946, p. 29; "Colleges for Women Admit Men," *Higher Education* 3 (15 December 1946): 8–9.

³⁰ For accreditation and other aspects of academic preparation for veterans, see Francis J. Brown, *Educational Opportunities for Veterans* (Washington: Public Affairs Press, 1946); Louis F. Batmale, "Veterans' High-School Graduation by Examination," *School Review* 56 (April 1948): 229–35; A. J. Brumbaugh, "Implications for Postwar Education of Credits for Military Experience," *North Central Association Quarterly* 19 (January 1945): 285–88; James D. Kline, "Specialized Counseling for Veterans at the University of Minnesota," *Educational Outlook* 22 (November 1947): 22–26; Earl J. McGrath, "The Procrustean Bed of Higher Education," *School and Society* 61 (10 February 1945): 81–84; George M. Wilcox, "College Credit to Veterans for Educational Experiences in the Armed Services," *School and Society* 68 (21 August 1948): 126–27; Earl J. McGrath, "Appraising the Veterans' Education," *Journal of Higher Education* 15 (October 1944): 343–50; Irving H. Anderson and William C. Morse, "The Reading of Veterans," *Journals of Higher Education* 17 (October 1946): 375–77; Byron H. Atkinson and Robert W. Webb, "Refresher Courses for Veterans," *Journal of Higher Education* 17 (October 1946): 377–80; George E. Wilkinson, "Orientation Interview for Veterans," *Journal of Higher Education* 20 (December 1949): 469–72.

³¹ For the General Educational Development Tests see E. F. Linquist, "The Use of Tests in the Accreditation of Military Experience and in the Educational Placement of War Veterans." *Education Record* 25 (October 1944): 357–76; for college and university acceptance of military credit see Wilcox, "College Credit to Veterans for Educational Experiences in the Armed Services"; and Brown, *Educational Opportunities for Veterans*, especially pp. 34–37; and Hillway, "G.I. Joe and the Colleges"; Paul Dressel and John Schmid, *An Evaluation of the Tests of General Educational Development*, American Council on Education, 1951; H. P. Wardlow, "The Use and Value of G.E.D. Tests for College Entrance of Veterans of the Armed Forces," *North Central Association Quarterly* 26 (January 1952): 295–301; Louis A. D'Amico, "The Scholastic Achievement of G.E.D. Students at Indiana University," *North Central Association Quarterly* 31 (January 1957): 256–59; for a description of the army universities see John Dale Russell, "Biarritz American University," *Higher Education* 2 (15 January 1946); and U.S. Army, *A History of Shrivenham American University*, 1946.

³² For glimpses of changes see W. T. Rolfe, "The Service Man Returns to the University of Texas," *Journal of the American Association of Collegiate Registrars* 20 (April 1945): 313–25; Robert K. Root, "Princeton Program for Servicemen," *Journal of Higher Education* 15 (December 1944): 455–58; Ernest V. Hollis and Ralph C. M. Flynt, *Higher Education Looks Ahead*, U.S. Office of Education Bulletin no. 8, 1945; "Manual for War Veterans," University of Illinois, n.d.; *New York Times*, 31 January 1946, p. 26; and Fine, *Democratic Education*, pp. 123–36.

³³ Under the amended legislation veterans had four (instead of two) years to commence and nine (rather than seven) to finish schooling (dated from discharge or the end of hostilities). Congress also voted to include correspondence courses under the program, authorized payment in excess of 500 dollars tuition and fees per year for short courses—with a corresponding reduction in the period of entitlement, deleted the clause that required

the amount paid under the education title to be deducted from any future bonus, and modified the basis for determining reasonable tuition rates for institutions whose tuition did not cover the cost of education (the V.A. would pay the cost of education, up to 500 dollars a year, if it exceeded tuition). See *United States Statutes At Large*, vol. 59, pt. 1, pp. 623–32.

[34] *New York Times*, 27 November 1945, p. 24; "The Progressives and the Veterans," *New Republic*, 22 October 1945, p. 516; also see "G.I. Graduate Students," *New Republic*, 26 November 1945, pp. 694–95; and Kyle Crichton, "G.I. Bill of Complaints," *Collier's*, 2 June 1945, pp. 14–15, 72.

[35] U.S., Congress, Senate, Committee on Finance, Subcommittee on Veterans' Legislation, *Hearings on H.R. 3749, Amendments to the Servicemen's Readjustment Act of 1944*, 79th Cong., 1st sess., 1945, p. 29.

[36] U.S., Congress, House, Committee on World War Veterans' Legislation, *Hearings on H.R. 3749 and Related Bills to Amend the Servicemen's Readjustment Act of 1944*, 79th Cong., 1st sess., 1945, p. 169.

[37] In addition to the Senate and House hearings, see "Great War–Legion Bill," folder 9, American Legion Library files; John Thomas Taylor, "Help for Joe," *American Legion Magazine* 39 (August 1945): 25, 30, 32; and Clarence Woodbury, "The Veterans' One-Man Lobby," *American Magazine* 141 (May 1946): 26–27, 123–26.

[38] House, *Hearings on H.R. 3749*, p. 109. Four years later, when the V.A. made a study of the G.I. Bill's operation, it reached the same conclusion Odom offered, that the 1945 amendments "obscured the original readjustment principle." See the statement by Carl R. Gray, Jr., Administrator of Veterans' Affairs, U.S., Congress, Senate, Committee on Labor and Public Welfare, *Report on Education and Training Under the Servicemen's Readjustment Act, As Amended*, 81st Cong., 2d sess., 1950, p. 12.

CHAPTER 3

[1] The statistics in this paragraph are from monthly V.A. reports, V.A. Research Division, Washington, D.C. (hereafter cited as VARD).

[2] Most sources round off the figures at 2,200,000; but see P. Timoshenko, controller, Division of Veterans Benefits, V.A., to Henry T. Tadd, 17 October 1960, in the file "Readjustment Training (P.L. 346)," VARD. Actually a few veterans, the beneficiaries of special administrative and legal proceedings, attended college under the World War II G.I. Bill as late as 1960. Officially, however, the program terminated in July 1956.

[3] Richard P. McCornick, *Rutgers: A Bicentennial History* (New Brunswick, N.J.: Rutgers University Press, 1966), p. 271; Omar N. Bradley, "The Colleges and the Veterans' Administration," *Association of American College Bulletins* 33 (March 1947): 44–50; Robert Preston Brooks, *The University of Georgia* (Athens: The University of Georgia Press, 1956), p. 234; *New York Times*, 22 September 1947, pp. 1, 26.

[4] U.S. Office of Education, "1948 Fall Enrollment In Higher Educational Institutions," Circular no. 248, 15 November 1948, Table F, p. 5.

[5] For these and other examples see *New York Times*, 10 January 1945, p. 25.

[6] "S.R.O.," *Time*, 18 March 1946, p. 75; *New York Times*, 13 January 1946; p. 38; 21 February 1946, p. 11. The G.I. Bill also permitted study outside the United States. During the spring of 1950, the peak of overseas popularity, 5,800 veterans studied in forty-five foreign countries. See *New York Times*, 6 May 1950, p. 13.

[7] Benjamin Fine, "Teachers Colleges No Longer Attract," *New York Times*, 16 February 1947, p. 45. For the problem of veterans gaining admission to the programs and schools of their choice, see *New York Times*, 26 May 1947, p. 23.

[8] U.S. Office of Education, "1948 Fall Enrollment in Higher Educational Institutions," Tables B and C, p. 3.

[9] The average annual increase 1930–1940 was 7,676 degrees; the increase 1920–1930 was 8,623.

[10] Norman Frederiksen and William B. Schrader, *Adjustment to College* (Princeton, N.J.: Educational Testing Service, 1951), p. 326. Also see John S. Allen, "Anticipated Demands for Higher Education," *School and Society* 66 (23 August 1947): 141. A survey at Clarkson College of Technology, on the other hand, found that fifty-five percent of the unmarried and seventy-three percent of the married veterans "would not have been able to attend college without aid from the G.I. Bill of Rights." See *New York Times*, 20 October 1946, IV, p. 13. Also, at the University of Iowa forty-eight percent of the veterans reported they would not be students "without G.I. Bill aid." See "Veterans at College," *Life*, 21 April 1947, pp. 112-13.

[11] George A. MacFarland, "Veterans at the University of Pennsylvania," *Educational Outlook* 22 (November 1947): 18; Curtis E. Avery, "Veterans' Education in the Universities," *Journal of Higher Education* 17 (October 1946): 360; Clifton L. Hall, "Veterans' Class, 1950," *School and Society* 73 (3 February 1951): 70; "The Class of 1949," *Fortune*, June 1949, p. 84; Benjamin Fine, "Educators Praise Their G.I. Students," *New York Times*, 11 October 1949, p. 35; Charles J. V. Murphy, "G.I.'s at Harvard," *Life*, 17 June 1946, p. 17.

[12] Edward C. McDonagh, "Adjustment Problems and Characteristics of University Veterans," *Sociology and Social Research* 31 (January 1947).

[13] Quoted by Benjamin Fine, "Veterans Raise College Standards," *Educational Outlook* 22 (November 1947): 58.

[14] MacFarland, "Veterans at the University of Pennsylvania," p. 18; Harry Estill More, "Campus Adjustment of Veterans," *Sociology and Social Research* 32 (January 1948): 713; also see John R. Kinzer, "The Veteran and Academic Adjustment," *Educational Research Bulletin* 25 (January 1946): 8-12; and William L. Painter and Helen W. Painter, "The Veteran as a College Freshmen," *Journal of Higher Education* 20 (11 January 1949): 42-45.

[15] Byron H. Atkinson, "Veteran vs. Non-Veteran Performance at UCLA," *Journal of Educational Research* 43 (December 1949): 302; Ronald B. Thompson and Marie A. Flesher, "Comparative Academic Records of Veterans and Civilian Students," *Journal of the American Association of Collegiate Registrars* 22 (January 1947): 179; Fine, "Veterans Raise College Standards," p. 54; "G.I. Grinds," *Newsweek*, 1 April 1946, p. 89; also see Clark Tibbitts and Woodrow W. Hunter, "Veterans and Non-Veterans at the University of Michigan," *School and Society* 65 (10 May 1947): 347-50; M. G. Orr, "Grade-Point Average of Veterans at Oklahoma Agricultural and Mechanical College," *School and Society* 66 (2 August 1947): 94; and Frederiksen and Schrader, *Adjustment to College*, pp. 7-10.

[16] Edith Efron, "Two Joes Meet: Joe College, Joe Veteran," *New York Times Magazine* 16 June 1946, p. 21; Ralph G. Martin, "The Best Is None too Good," *New Republic*, 26 August 1946, p. 227; Fine, "Veterans Raise College Standards," pp. 54-61.

[17] For a study that found nonveterans earned slightly higher grades than veterans, see Robert H. Farber and Lawrence Riggs, "Veterans in a Privately Endowed Liberal Arts College, 1946-1950," *School and Society* 72 (12 August 1950): 105-6.

[18] Edgar A. Taylor, Jr., "How Well Are Veterans Doing?" *School and Society* 65 (22 March 1947): 213.

[19] *New York Times*, 1 January 1946, p. 23; Fine, "Veterans Raise College Standards," p. 54; also see Ruth G. Weintraub and Ruth E. Salley, "Hunter College Reports on Its Veterans," *School and Society* 68 (24 July 1948): 63; Allan P. Farrell, "Report on the Veterans," *America*, 12 April 1947, p. 1.

[20] Arthur M. Gowan, "Characteristics of Freshmen Veterans," *Journal of Higher Education* 20 (April 1949): 205; Edward L. Clark, "Veteran as a College Freshman," *School and Society* 66 (13 September 1947): 207; Jean M. Crose and Norman W. Garmezy, "A Comparison of the Academic Achievement of Matched Groups of Veteran and Non-Veteran Freshmen at the University of Iowa," *Journal of Educational Research* 41 (March 1948): 547-50.

[21] For a sample, see L. L. Love and C. A. Hutchison, "Academic Progress of Veterans,"

Educational Research Bulletin 25 (November 1946): 223–26; "Academic Achievements of Veterans at Cornell University," *School and Society* 65 (8 February 1947): 101–2; Frederick D. Pultz, "Veterans in the Ohio State University College of Education," *Educational Research Bulletin* 26 (September 1947): 153–56; and Louis M. Hansen and Donald G. Paterson, "Scholastic Achievement of Veterans," *School and Society* 69 (12 March 1949): 195–97.

[22] Frederiksen and Schrader, *Adjustment to College,* p. 13; Irving C. Whittemore, "Does a Military Interruption Decrease the Chances of Obtaining a Degree?" *School and Society* 78 (25 July 1953): 25–27.

[23] Frederiksen and Schrader, *Adjustment to College,* pp. 63, 93–96, 180–83, 247, 14.

[24] Ibid., p. 235.

[25] "The reason for going to college most often given by nonveterans was to get necessary training for entering a profession; veterans most often said they wished to prepare themselves for a better-paying job." See ibid., p. 255.

[26] Ibid., pp. 255–57, 308–9, 352.

[27] Ibid., p. 219. Also see Harry D. Gideonse, "Educational Achievement of Veterans at Brooklyn College: A Study of the Performance of Some 2400 Veterans in the Period from 1946 to 1949," *Educational Record* 31 (October 1950): 453–68; Robert H. Shaffer, "Note on the Alleged Scholastic Superiority of Veterans," *School and Society* 67 (13 March 1948): 205; William A. Owens and William A. Owens, Jr., "Some Factors in the Academic Superiority of Veteran Students," *Journal of Educational Psychology* 40 (December 1949): 499–502.

[28] "Less than half thought that ability to do college work was increased as a consequence of military service, while about a fourth thought ability was decreased. . . . Students with high grades presumably tended to attribute their success in part to service experience, while students with low grades tended to blame service experience for their poor standing." See Frederiksen and Schrader, *Adjustment to College,* pp. 204, 213.

[29] Ibid., pp. 196, 198, 214.

[30] Ibid., pp. 326–27.

[31] Ibid., p. 48. In their systematic study of veterans attending Ohio State University, Thompson and Pressey "concluded that the superior record of the veterans is a complex product of maturity, wide experience, motivation, and relative freedom from financial needs." See Ronald B. Thompson and S. L. Pressey, "Analysis of the Academic Records of 2,144 Veterans," *College and University* 23 (January 1948): 252.

CHAPTER 4

[1] U.S., Congress, House, *Report of the House Select Committee To Investigate Educational and Training Program under G.I. Bill,* 81st Cong., 2d sess., 1951, H. R. 3253, p. 7; also see file titled "Sections J-K-L Misc. and Personnel (*Time Series*)," Vocational Rehabilitation and Education Division, Veterans Administration.

[2] U.S., Congress, House, *Management Survey of Activities of the Veterans Administration by the Firm of Booz-Allen-Hamilton,* 82d Cong., 2d sess., 1952, H. Print 322, pp. 8, 101–16, 826, 833–34, 840, and 844.

[3] U.S., Congress, House, Committee on Veterans' Affairs, *Hearings on Education and Training and Other Benefits for Veterans Serving on or after June 27, 1950,* 82d Cong., 2d sess., 1952, p. 1352; 81st Cong., 2d sess., H. R. 3253, p. 6; U.S., Congress, House, *The President's Commission on Veterans' Pensions, A Report on Veterans' Benefits in the United States, Staff Report IX, Part B: Readjustment Benefits: Education and Training, and Employment and Unemployment,* 84th Cong., 2d sess., 1956, H. Print 291, p. 115.

[4] The V.A. ruled that an "ordinary school year" consisted of two semesters or three quarters of not less than thirty nor more than thirty-eight weeks, and that a "full-time" course of study was a minimum of twelve hours per semester or its equivalent on a quarter system.

⁵ U.S., Congress, House, *General Accounting Office Report of Survey—Veterans' Education and Training Program,* 82d Cong., 1st sess., 1951, H. Print 160, p. 7; U.S., Congress, Senate, Committee on Labor and Public Welfare, Subcommittee on Veterans, *Hearings on Bills Relating to Education and On-the-Job Training Programs for Veterans,* 80th Cong., 1st sess., 1947, p. 251 (hereafter cited as Senate Subcommittee, *Hearings on Bills Relating to Education).*

⁶ Public Law 610, 13 July 1950 authorized the V.A. to require guidance for a veteran wishing to make a second change in his field of study.

⁷ 84th Cong., 2d sess., H. Print 291, pp. 67–72; "Situation Abnormal," *School and Society* 67 (6 March 1948): 184; Alan O. Dech and Prentice Reeves, "Effects of Advisement upon Continuation in Training under P.L. 346," *School and Society* 67 (5 June 1948): 429–31; James D. Kline, "A University Meets the Veterans' Needs," *Educational Record* 28 (April 1947): 190–206; Mitchell Dreese, "Policies and Plans of College Guidance Centers Operating under VA Contracts," *Educational Record* 30 (October 1949): 446–57; and *Information Bulletin 7–20,* 19 November 1946, and *Consolidated Monthly Reports,* Vocational Rehabilitation and Education Division, V.A.

⁸ December 1945 Congress amended the law to permit the V.A. to pay tuition at a rate in excess of $500 with a proportionate reduction in the veteran's period of eligibility.

⁹ See *New York Times,* 3 December 1945, p. 23; 5 December 1945, p. 26; and 18 December 1945, p. 18.

¹⁰ One college increased its nonresident tuition from $25 to $100 per quarter although the original figure represented the estimated cost of instruction. In this case the V.A. recovered from the college $340,000 in overpayment. See 82nd Cong., 1st sess., H. Print 160, p. 5.

¹¹ For details on the tuition problem see U.S., Congress, House, *Investigating Education and Training Programs under G.I. Bill,* 82d Cong., 2d sess., 1952. H. R. 1375, pp. 60–80; 84th Cong., 2d sess., H. Print 291, pp. 75–82; 82d Cong., 1st sess., H. Print 160, pp. 5–6, 10, 70–79; and A. H. Monk, "New Chapter in Tuition Payments for Veterans," *Higher Education* 6 (1 October 1949): 25–27.

¹² 82d Cong., 1st sess., H. Print 160, pp. 6–7.

¹³ 84th Cong., 2d sess., H. Print 291, 82d Cong., 2d sess., H. R. p. 75 n32; 1375, pp. 221, 4, 10–12, 19; U.S., Congress, House, *Report on Education and Training under the Servicemen's Readjustment Act, as amended, from the Administrator of Veterans Affairs,* 81st Cong., 2d sess., 1950, H. Print 210, p. 9; 84th Cong., 2d sess., H. Print 291, pp. 24, 30, 117.

¹⁴ 82d Cong., 2d sess., H. Print 1375, especially pp. 12, 18–19; 82d Cong., 1st sess., H. Print 160, p. 53.

¹⁵ For example, see "No Hobos," *Time,* 26 August 1946, p. 77; *New York Times,* 15 August 1946, p. 44.

¹⁶ See World War II G.I. Bill file, Harry S. Truman Papers, Truman Library; *New York Times,* 12 January 1947, p. 37. For an official survey made by Congressman W. Howes Meade see "Financial Needs of Veterans," *School and Society* 66 (13 September 1947): 198.

¹⁷ For the position on subsistence increases that the Legion, VA, AVC, ACE, university officials, and individual veterans took, see U.S., Congress, House, Committee on Veterans' Affairs, Subcommittee on Education, Training, and Rehabilitation, *Hearings on Bills to Increase Subsistence Allowance Rates,* 80th Cong., 1st sess., 1947 (hereafter cited as House Subcommittee, *Hearings on Bills to Increase Subsistence);* U.S., Congress, House, Committee on Veterans' Affairs, *Hearings to Increase Subsistence Allowance Rates,* 80th Cong., 1st sess., 1947; and Senate Subcommittee, *Hearings on Bills Relating to Education,* May-June 1947.

¹⁸ Senate Subcommittee, *Hearings on Bills Relating to Education,* 6 May 1947, p. 30; House Subcommittee, *Hearings on Bills to Increase Subsistence,* 21 March 1947, p. 10. For the V.A. position see statements by Omar N. Bradley, V.A. administrator, U.S., Congress, Senate, *Providing Increased Subsistence Allowance to Veterans Pursuing Certain Courses under*

The Servicemen's Readjustment Act of 1944, as Amended, 80th Cong., 1st sess., 1947, S. R. 420, p. 2; Senate Subcommittee, *Hearings on Bills Relating to Education,* 5 May 1947, p. 5; and Carl R. Gray, Jr. (Bradley's successor) to James E. Webb, 11 February 1948, World War II G.I. Bill file, Truman Papers.

[19] Richard O. Davies, *Housing Reform during the Truman Administration* (Columbia: University of Missouri Press, 1966), p. 41; *New York Times,* 6 January 1945, p. 1; ibid., 9 June 1946, VI, p. 11.

[20] U.S., Congress, House, *Independent Offices Appropriation Bill, 1950,* 81st Cong., 1st sess., 1949, H. R. 425, p. 21; "Pop Goes to College," *Newsweek,* 26 November 1945, pp. 104–5; *New York Times,* 5 July 1946, p. 19. For a brief summary of the Reuse Program see U.S., Housing and Home Finance Agency, *Third Annual Report* (Washington: Government Printing Office, 1950), pt. 4, chap. 5, but especially pp. 344–45.

[21] "Can Married Ex-Service Man Afford College?" *Higher Education* 1 (15 March 1945): 11; *New York Times,* 6 February 1946, p. 11; 14 April 1946, p. 11; 6 May 1946, p. 23; and 18 June 1946, p. 15.

[22] In June 1948 Congress relinquished to the colleges all contractual rights with respect to temporary veterans housing.

[23] Public Law 697, 8 August 1946, 79th Congress.

[24] In practice this meant institutions of higher learning. The annual reports of the Federal Works Agency occasionally substituted "colleges" for "educational institutions."

[25] The colleges reerected and remodeled 975 of these structures at their own expense.

[26] U.S., Federal Works Agency, *Eighth Annual Report, 1947* (Washington: Government Printing Office, 1947), pp. 35–41; ibid., *Ninth Annual Report, 1948,* pp. 30–33; ibid., *Tenth Annual Report, 1949,* pp. 116–19; Dillon S. Myer, "Colleges and the Housing Crises," *Higher Education* 3 (15 November 1946): 2.

[27] To help a tiny fraction of the ablest high school graduates attend college the state maintained a scholarship program. But since the recipients of the scholarship had to attend New York State colleges the program seemed designed to aid the private schools at least as much as to aid the students. Despite this program, New York State ranked last among the forty-eight states in state expenditures for higher education per youth, eighteen to twenty-four, and last in state expenditures for higher education relative to per capita income. See J. Hillis Miller and John S. Allen, *Veterans Challenge the Colleges* (New York: King's Crown Press, 1947), p. 134.

[28]

	October 1941	November 1946
11 teachers colleges	5,897	7,803
University of Rochester	2,147	3,706
Syracuse University	5,450	11,483
R.P.I.	1,427	3,308

Potsdam, New York, twelve miles south of the Canadian border, had both a teachers college (named after the town) and a private engineering college (Clarkson), while twenty miles west in Canton was St. Lawrence University. Between 1941 and 1946, enrollment at Potsdam climbed 8 percent; at Clarkson College, 137 percent; and at St. Lawrence, 170 percent. The November 1946 enrollment at St. Lawrence exceeded its 1943 total capacity inventory by 451 students. Clarkson's later enrollment exceeded its earlier capacity by 639 students. But in November 1946 Potsdam State Teachers College still needed 221 students to reach its capacity. See Miller and Allen, *Veterans Challenge the Colleges,* pp. 83–86.

[29] In October 1941 there were 102,847 full-time college students in New York State. The state's 1943 capacity inventory concluded that 146,000 students could squeeze onto the state's campuses. In March 1946 Dewey and educators expected enrollment to reach 200,000.

[30] Tolley to Stoddard, 15 February 1946, reprinted in Amy M. Gilbert, *Associated Colleges of Upper New York* (Ithaca: Cornell University Press, 1950), pp. 24–25.

[31] For the creation and operation of ACUNY see Gilbert, *Associated Colleges of Upper*

New York; Miller and Allen, *Veterans Challenge the Colleges;* G. Baily, "First G.I. University: Champlain College," *New York Times Magazine,* 6 October 1946, pp. 6–7; and *New York Times,* 8 March 1946, p. 38.

³² Quoted by Frank C. Abbott, *Government Policy and Higher Education* (Ithaca: Cornell University Press, 1958), p. 282.

³³ Syracuse University founded Harpur College in 1946 as an extension center. SUNY absorbed Harpur in 1950 when Syracuse economized because of declining enrollments and income.

³⁴ For the creation of SUNY see Abbott, *Government Policy and Higher Education,* pp. 194–323; and Oliver Cromwell Carmichael, Jr., *New York State Establishes a State University* (Nashville: Vanderbilt University Press, 1955).

³⁵ *Historical Statistics of the United States, Colonial Times to 1957* (U.S. Bureau of the Census, 1960), p. 210; John D. Millett, *Financing Higher Education in the United States* (New York: Columbia University Press, 1952), p. 116; college income from tuition and fees between 1939–1940 and 1949–1950 increased only slightly more than over-all college budgets; see Simon and Grant, *Digest of Educational Statistics 1968,* p. 95; Millett, *Financing Higher Education in the United States,* p. 116.

³⁶ Louis G. Geiger, *University of the Northern Plains* (Grand Forks: University of North Dakota Press, 1958), p. 410; Richard P. McCormick, *Rutgers: A Bicentennial History* (New Brunswick, N.J.: Rutgers University Press, 1966), p. 273.

³⁷ *New York Times,* 17 November 1946, IV, p. 9; G. Wallace Chessman, *Denison: The Story of an Ohio College* (Granville, Ohio: Denison University, 1957), p. 345; also see "Are the Veterans a Financial Burden?" *School and Society* 65 (22 February 1947): 136; George H. Callcott, *A History of the University of Maryland* (Baltimore: Maryland Historical Society, 1966), p. 339.

³⁸ Benjamin Fine, "College at Brown University for Veterans without Credits Proves a Great Success," *New York Times,* 13 April 1947, p. 9.

³⁹ Comparative statistics: 1946, 35.2 percent vs 51.9 percent; 1947, 40.5 percent vs 52.1 percent; see James A. Atkins, "Negro Educational Institutions and the Veterans' Educational Facilities Program," *Journal of Negro Education* 17 (Spring 1948): 144.

⁴⁰ Except for the figures in the above note, all education statistics are from *Biennial Survey of Education in the United States, 1938–1940,* vol. 2, chap. 1, p. 38; and ibid., *1948–1950,* chap. 1, p. 50. For the Negro colleges see Atkins, "Negro Educational Institutions and the Veterans' Educational Facilities Program," pp. 141–53; Markin D. Jenkins, "Significant Programs in Institutions of Higher Learning of Negroes," *Educational Record* 26 (October 1945): 301–11; Charles H. Tompson, "Editorial Comment: Some Critical Aspects of the Problem of the Higher and Professional Education for Negroes," *Journal of Negro Education* 14 (Fall 1945): 509–26; Benjamin Quarles, "The Background of the 1947 College Student," *Quarterly Review of Higher Education among Negroes* 15 (April 1947): 87–90; and I. A. Derbigny, "Tuskegee Looks at Its Veterans," ibid., 14 (January 1946): 11–18.

¹⁴ *Information Bulletin 7–106,* 6 June 1956, p. 16, Vocational Rehabilitation and Education Division, V.A.; Olive Remington Goldman, "College Student, G.I. Style," *Journal of the American Association of University Women* 39 (June 1946): 205; G. A. MacFarland, "Veterans at the University of Pennsylvania," *Educational Outlook* 22 (November 1947): 16; Byron H. Atkinson, "Social and Financial Adjustment of Veterans at UCLA," *School and Society* 72 (8 July 1950): 24. For other examples of age see "Veteran Students at the University of Minnesota," ibid. 64 (23 November 1946): 360; Ronald B. Thompson and Sidney L. Pressey, "Analysis of the Academic Records of 2,144 Veterans," *College and University* 23 (January 1948): 251; and Donald D. Stewart and Richard P. Chambers, "The Status Background of the Veteran College Student," *Sociology and Social Research* 35 (September 1950): 16.

⁴² *Information Bulletin 7–106,* 6 June 1956, p. 18, Vocational Rehabilitation and Education Division, V.A. In May 1947 the American Council on Education completed a study which found thirty-five percent of veteran-students married." See Senate Subcommittee, *Hearings on Bills Relating to Education,* p. 246.

⁴³ *New York Times,* 24 April 1946, p. 31; "Married Undergrads," *Time,* 10 December 1945, p. 70; and Milton Mackaye, "Crisis at the Colleges," *Saturday Evening Post,* 3 August 1946, p. 36.
⁴⁴ In addition to ibid., see Billie W. Duke, "This Is the House the Dukes Built," *Woman's Home Companion,* January 1947, pp. 86–87; Amy Porter, "The G.I. Villagers," *Collier's,* 18 October 1947, pp. 12–13; Virginia Messenger, "Veterans' Families Go to School," *Journal of Home Economics* 42 (June 1950): 431–34; "The University," *Harvard Alumni Bulletin* 49 (28 September 1946), pp. 9–16; and *New York Times,* 19 February 1946, p. 28; 28 February 1946, p. 25; 22 September 1946, VI, p. 22; 1 September 1947, p. 12.
⁴⁵ Mary L. Dee, "We Live in G.I. Town," *Coronet,* July 1952, p. 66; Judson T. Landis, "On the Campus," *Survey Midmonthly* 84 (January 1948): 17; "Veterans at College," *Life,* 21 April 1947, p. 112; for married life also see ibid., 7 January 1946, pp. 37–38; John Paul Jones, "Learning Life in a Vet Village," *Christian Science Monitor Magazine,* 19 October 1946, p. 7; Hildegarde Dolson, "Parking Double," *Ladies' Home Journal,* June 1947, pp. 209–14; C. S. Forester, "Meet a Student Veteran," ibid., May 1945, pp. 137–40, 163; and Barbara Gunn, "Graduation: Family Style," *Saturday Evening Post,* 15 May 1948, pp. 18–19.
⁴⁶ At the State University of Iowa only one percent of the veterans answered yes to the question, "Can you get along on your G.I. Money?" "Veterans at College," *Life,* 21 April 1947, pp. 112–13; *New York Times,* 6 April 1947, p. 54; 27 June 1947, p. 23; "Expenditures by Veterans at Stanford," *Higher Education* 3 (15 January 1947): 7; House Subcommittee, *Hearings on Bills to Increase Subsistence.*
⁴⁷ "Veterans at College," *Life,* 21 April 1947, p. 109; *New York Times,* 27 June 1947, p. 3; "Expenditures by Veterans at Stanford," p. 7; and Landis, "On the Campus," p. 19.

CHAPTER 5

¹ In December 1945 the faculty eliminated the differential between war credits granted enlisted men and officers. Thereafter both groups received fifteen credits. War credits did not apply to Graduate, Law, or Medical Schools, and applied to engineering and pharmacy students only by special permission. *Daily Cardinal,* 6 November 1945, p. 1; 1 December 1945, p. 4; and 4 December 1945, p. 1.
² *The University of Wisconsin Press Bulletin,* 23 February 1944, p. 1, box 3, file 5/11, University of Wisconsin Archives.
³ "General Information for Veterans," undated mimeographed pamphlet, and an undated typed manuscript from the files of Douglas A. Dixon, Veterans Counselor, University of Wisconsin; *Bulletin of the University of Wisconsin,* 1945, pp. 16–17; Bulletin, Office of Veterans Affairs, November 1945, box 3, file 5/11, University of Wisconsin Archives; *Daily Cardinal,* 18 October 1945, p. 1; 10 January 1946, p. 7; and 24 January 1946, p. 1.
⁴ Report of Office of the Personnel Council by Edward E. Milligan, 4 August 1945; Dixon to Martha E. Peterson, 4 April 1966; Milligan to R. W. Bolling, 24 July 1946; typed manuscript, "Office of Veterans Affairs," 27 February 1948—all in Dixon files; Office of Veterans Affairs Bulletin, November 1945, box 3, file 5/11, University of Wisconsin Archives.
⁵ *Daily Cardinal,* 24 January 1946, pp. 1, 7; 30 October 1946, p. 1.
⁶ E. B. Fred, "Dear Badger in Service," p. 3, box 3, file 5/11, University of Wisconsin Archives; Marion Wilhelm, "University Can House Only 12,500 Next Fall," *Daily Cardinal,* 9 January 1946, p. 1; *Daily Cardinal,* 1 November 1946, p. 6; 16 November 1946, p. 5; 7 February 1947, p. 1; *1945–47 Biennial Report of the President,* December, 1946, p. 50, University of Wisconsin Archives; *Daily Cardinal,* 7 October 1947, p. 1.
⁷ From a low in 1946 of 10.5 percent in Graduate School and 4.2 percent in Law

and Medicine, enrollment climbed to 20.8 percent and to 6.9 percent, respectively, in 1951 and then dropped off.

⁸ The 1945 figure was only partly the effect of war: in 1930 the figure was 28 percent. The percentage of foreign students, however, increased steadily: from 1.3 percent in 1946 to 2.5 percent in 1950 to 4.3 percent in 1959. *Facts about the University of Wisconsin,* no. 16, box 1, file 29/00/5, University of Wisconsin Archives; Lins Papers, file 19/11/3/00–1, University of Wisconsin Archives.

⁹ *Daily Cardinal,* 7 July 1944, p. 1; 1 February 1945, p. 4; also see ibid., 30 March 1946, p. 4.

¹⁰ Lawrence O'Neill, Jr., "There Is No 'Vet Problem' at Madison," *The Wisconsin Alumnus* 48 (January 1947): 12–13, 28, 30.

¹¹ *Daily Cardinal,* 29 March 1946, p. 1; 24 September 1946, p. 1; 9 May 1947, p. 1; 27 November 1947, p. 1; Lins Papers, file 19/11/3/00–1, University of Wisconsin Archives.

¹² Leslie E. Martin, Jr., "A Comparative Study of Veterans' Academic Achievement before and after Service," unpublished graduate seminar paper, Lins Papers, file 19/11/3/ 00–1, University of Wisconsin Archives. Seven of nine who earned lower grades, however, recorded a change of under 0.3 of a grade point.

¹³ *Daily Cardinal,* 2 October 1947, p. 1; also see editorial, ibid., 28 October 1947, 4; ibid., 13 December 1945, p. 1; Theodore W. Zillman to John N. Andrews, 23 July 1947, Dixon files; E. E. Milligan to John N. Andrews, 5 February 1946, Dixon files; Kenneth Little, "Student Personnel Problems," *College and University* 23 (October 1947): 64.

¹⁴ In 1949–1950, 61.7 percent of the veterans pursued careers in the liberal arts while only 1.4 percent registered in the School of Commerce. Comparable statistics for the nonveterans were 51 percent and 4.5 percent.

¹⁵ *Report of the President for the Year 1949–1950,* Madison, 1951, p. 8; also see *Report of the President for the Biennium 1947–1949,* Madison, 1950, pp. 12, 13, both in University of Wisconsin Archives.

¹⁶ Tax-supported colleges and universities repeated this practice across the country.

¹⁷ *Daily Cardinal,* 8 January 1946, p. 1; 16 March 1948, p. 5; 3 May 1949, p. 1; 22 February 1951, p. 5.

¹⁸ Of the $1,469,000 total cost, the federal government paid $790,000. *Daily Cardinal,* 20 September 1946, p. 1; 22 January 1947, p. 1; 1 April 1947, p. 1; 27 September 1947, p. 6; 18 October 1947, p. 1.

¹⁹ *Wisconsin Alumnus* 46 (15 February 1945): 4.

²⁰ Quoted in *Daily Cardinal,* 7 November 1947, p. 8.

²¹ *Daily Cardinal,* 15 January 1948, p. 1; 3 May 1949, pp. 1, 10.

²² *Report of the President for the Year 1949–1950,* May 1951, Madison, pp. 9, 18.

²³ For a list of buildings and their financing, see ibid., p. 23.

²⁴ "Randall Park," *Wisconsin Alumnus* 47 (20 October 1945): 9, Phyliss Ashmun, "Vetsburg Housing Thrills Veterans' Wives, Children," *Daily Cardinal,* 25 September 1945, p. 1; Marvin Riley and Svend Riemer, "Trailer Communities on a University Campus," *Journal of Land and Public Utility Economics* 23 (February 1947): 81–83.

²⁵ *Daily Cardinal,* 20 September 1946, p. 1; Mueller to Board of Regents, 30 January 1948, file 24/6/1, University of Wisconsin Archives.

²⁶ For Truax see *Daily Cardinal,* especially 19 December 1946, p. 1; 9 March 1948, p. 1; James Dugan, "Traux Field Units Come to Rescue of Homeless Servicemen Students," 7 February 1946, p. 1; and box 1, file 25/8/1, University of Wisconsin Archives.

²⁷ Although the university provided services from the start, it did not gain legal control of the project until December 1946.

²⁸ For Badger Village see box 1, file 25/7/1; boxes 3, 5, and 6, file 25/7/2; and boxes 2 and 3, file 25/7/3—all University of Wisconsin Archives; E. B. Fred, "The University and the G.I.," *Wisconsin Alumnus* 48 (September–October 1946): 3–4; *Daily Cardinal,* especially, "Badger Village Closes Successful Life," 1 July 1952, p. 1.

[29] See Theodore W. Zillman, "Fraternities: One Current Evaluation," *Banta's Greek Exchange*, October 1963, pp. 266–70, found in files of Peter Bun, Student Organization Adviser, University of Wisconsin; *Daily Cardinal*, 7 December 1945, p. 4; 20 December 1945, p. 4; 30 November 1946, p. 9; and 24 October 1947, p. 7.

[30] *Daily Cardinal*, 29 November 1944, p. 1; 27 March 1945, p. 1.

[31] Ibid., 24 November 1946, p. 7.

[32] Shirley Kast, "U.W. Vets' Club: Phoney or Legit?" ibid., 14 February 1947, p. 1; 15 February 1947, p. 1; also see editorial 18 February 1947, p. 4.

[33] *Daily Cardinal*, 15 February 1947, p. 1.

[34] Ibid., 27 February 1947, p. 1.

[35] *Summer Cardinal*, 5 July 1946, p. 1.

[36] Ibid., 6 July 1947, p. 1.

[37] *Daily Cardinal*, 24 April 1947, p. 1; 20 February 1947, p. 1.

[38] Ibid., 21 September 1949, p. 4; 9 January 1951, p. 4.

[39] As one veteran observed, "The conclusion is inescapable that we're getting short changed," but he added, "Wisconsin is probably just as good or better in comparison with most American schools." Mort Levine to editor, ibid., 15 February 1949, p. 4.

CHAPTER 6

[1] For brevity and constitutional correctness I will write in the rest of this chapter that Congress wrote and passed the 1944 G.I. Bill. In chapter 1 I discuss the Legion's contribution to passage of the act.

[2] For the 1948 figures see "1948 Fall Enrollment in Higher Educational Institutions," U.S. Office of Education, Circular No. 248, 15 November 1948, plus letters to me from several university archives. For the 1968 figures see Kenneth A. Simon and W. Vance Grant, *Digest of Educational Statistics 1968* (Washington: Government Printing Office, 1968), p. 85.

[3] For examples of these criticisms see D. D. Feder, "When Colleges Bulge," *College and University* 23 (October 1947): 116; Jud Kinberg, "Faults on Both Sides," *The American Scholar* 16 (Summer 1947): 347; Robert Wheeler, "A Social Problem to Be Faced," ibid., p. 349; George N. Constable, "Sophomore Looks at Education," *South Atlantic Quarterly* 47 (April 1948): 164–72; and the University of Wisconsin's *Daily Cardinal*, 15 April and 18 May 1949, p. 4.

[4] John Higham, "Subsidy or Sympathy?" *American Scholar* 16 (Summer 1947): 343.

[5] Cecil F. Rospaw, "The Need for Flexibility," ibid., p. 351.

[6] U.S., Congress, House, *Education and Training and Other Benefits for Persons Serving in the Armed Forces on or After June 27, 1950*, 82d Cong., 2d sess., 1952, H. R. 1943, p. 22.

[7] U.S., Congress, House, *Report of the House Select Committee to Investigate Educational and Training Program under G.I. Bill*, 81st Cong., 2d sess., 1951, H. R. 3253; U.S., Congress, House, *Investigating Education and Training Programs Under G.I. Bill*, 82d Cong., 2d sess., 1952, H. R. 1375; U.S., Congress, House, *General Accounting Office Report of Survey-Veterans' Education and Training Program*, 82d Cong., 1st sess., 1951, H. Print 160; and U.S., Congress, House, *Report on Education and Training under the Servicemen's Readjustment Act, as Amended, from the Administrator of Veterans Affairs*, 81st Cong., 2d sess., 1950, H. Print 210.

[8] U.S., Congress, Senate, Committee on Labor and Public Welfare, *Hearings on Certain Educational and Training Benefits to Veterans*, 82d Cong., 1st sess., 17, 18, 19, September 1951; and U.S., Congress, House, Committee on Veterans' Affairs, *Hearings on Education and Training and Other Benefits for Veterans Serving on or after June 27, 1950*, 32d Cong., 2d sess., 1952.

[9] Later in its report the association uses only the $800 figure.

[10] 82 Cong., 2d sess., H. R. 1375, pp. 74–75, 76, 78–79.

[11] 82d Cong., 2d sess., H.R. 1943, p. 26.

[12] The Teague Committee reported (p. 15) that "nothing in the form of a concrete over-all recommendation has been received from any of the national veterans' organizations."

[13] U.S., Congress, House, Committee on Veterans' Affairs, *Hearings on Legislation to Provide G.I. Bill Benefits for Post-Korean Veterans*, 89th Cong., 1st sess., 1965, pp. 3091, 3093, 2907, 2901.

[14] Cyril F. Brickfield, "The G.I. Bill Paid Off," *Employment Service Review* (June–July 1965), reprinted in *G.I. Benefits For Post-Korean Veterans*, 89th Cong., 1st sess., 1965, pp. 2916–17; also see letter from W. J. Driver, administrator, Veterans' Administration, to Teague, 19 January 1966, reprinted in U.S., Congress, House, Committee on Veterans' Affairs, *Hearings on Legislation to Provide G.I. Bill Benefits for Post-Korean Veterans*, 89th Cong., 2d sess., 1966, pp. 3107–8.

[15] *G.I. Bill Benefits for Post-Korean Veterans*, 89th Cong., 2d sess., 1966, pp. 3107–3108; for additional V.A. recognition of the relationship between potential veteran unemployment and the G.I. Bills, see Brickfield's article in *G.I. Bill Benefits for Post-Korean Veterans*, 89th Cong., 1st sess., 1965, pp. 2916–17.

[16] *G.I. Bill Benefits for Post-Korean Veterans*, 89th Cong., 1st sess., 1965, p. 2952.

[17] *G.I. Bill Benefits for Post-Korean Veterans*, 89th Cong., 2d sess., 1966, p. 3107; and *G.I. Bill Benefits for Post-Korean Veterans*, 89th Cong., 1st sess., 1965, p. 2971.

[18] Truman to each member of the commission, 13 July 1946, *Higher Education for American Democracy* (Washington: Government Printing Office, 1947), 5 vol.; also see John Snyder, *The Veteran and Higher Education* (Washington: Government Printing Office, 1946), p. 39.

[19] The commission also called for an end to discrimination by "race, creed, sex, or national origins."

[20] Gail Kennedy, ed., *Education for Democracy* (Boston: D.C. Heath and Company, 1952).

[21] Veterans Administration Press Release, 21 June 1964, p. 2.

[22] 82d Cong., 2d sess., H. R. 1375, p. 79.

[23] "The Fortune Survey," *Fortune*, (September 1949 Supplement), p. 4.

Index

AFL-CIO, 107
Alabama Polytechnic Institute, 76
Alfgren, Lee, 94
Alfred University, 69, 71
Allen, John S., 41
Allen, Leonard, 37
American Association of Teachers
  Colleges, 23
American Council on Education (ACE):
  and plan for benefits, 13, 23;
  cooperation with PMC and Osborn
  Committee, 14; and "Committee on
  Relationships of Higher Education to
  the Federal Government," 14; and G.I.
  Bill, 22; sponsors conference, 23;
  publications, 34–35; supports V.A., 61;
  and increases in subsistence payments,
  65; and classroom and other building
  shortages, 67; and veteran housing, 76
American Legion: as pressure group, 3, 4;
  concern over veteran demobilization, 4;
  campaign for legislation, 12, 15;
  contribution to G.I. Bill, 18–19;
  motivation of, 20, 101, 102; persons
  with similar opinions, 21; mentioned,
  22, 107; claims credit for G.I. Bill, 24;
  present when Roosevelt signed G.I. Bill,
  27; supports liberalization of G.I. Bill
  (1945), 37; and liberalization of G.I. Bill,
  38–39; and subsistence increases, 65;
  David Schreiner Post, No. 520, 95; calls
  for Vietnam G.I. Bill, 107; cites success
  of World War II G.I. Bill, 107; opposes
  "Cold War G.I. Bill," 108. See also
  Legion bill
American Veterans Committee (AVC),
  38, 64–65, 95–96
American Youth for Democracy, 96
Armed Forces Committee on Post-war
  Educational Opportunities for Service
  Personnel. See Osborn Committee
Army University Study Centers, 35
Arnold, Samuel T., 74
Associated Colleges of Upper New York
  (ACUNY), 70–71
Association of Land-Grant Colleges and
  Universities, 106
Atherton, Warren H., 1, 15, 18, 19, 20
Atkinson, Byron H., 50
Avery, Curtis, 49

Barden, Graham A., 23
Barkley, Alben W., 119 n.35
Baughman, Cortlandt C., 10, 11
Berg, William W., 99
Blaesser, W. W., 85
Bolte, Charles G., 28
Boston College, 43
Bradley, Omar N., 37
Brickfield, Cyril F., 108
Brown, Francis J., 6, 13, 25, 32, 33, 61, 65
Brown University, 73–74
Brumbaugh, A. J., 33
Byrnes, James F., 29, 30

"Canadian Preparations for Veterans'
  Demobilization and Rehabilitation,"
  7–8, 15
Carnegie Commission on Higher
  Education (1970), 110
Carnegie Foundation for the
  Advancement of Teaching, 52
Cejnar, Jack, 16
Central College (Fayette, Missouri), 45
Champlain College, 70, 72
Civilian Conservation Corps (CCC), 24,
  29, 101
City College of New York (CCNY), 62,
  77, 78
Clark, Edward L., 51
Clark, Joel Bennett (Champ), 16, 17, 19,
  21, 22, 38
Clark bill. See Legion bill
Clarkson College of Technology,
  125 n.10, 128 n.28
Colgate University, 35, 70
Colmery, Harry, 20, 119 n.35
Columbia University, 51, 69, 77
Conant, James B., 33, 38, 49
Cornell University, 14, 69, 70, 71
Crose, Jean M., 52

Daily Cardinal, 79, 84, 91, 96–97
Dartmouth College, 77
Davis, Burton, 117 n.8
Delano, Frederick A., 4, 5
"Demobilization and Readjustment," 8–9.
  See also PMC
Denison University, 73
Department of Defense, 108, 110
DePauw University, 45